The Conference for Leaders

A story featuring the Great 8 Leadership Principles, recognizable scenarios, ROI (return on investment) thinking and 100% applicability.

"Add this to your desktop collection of leadership solutions!"

Doug Booker

and

Terrell L. McTyer • Debra Hayes • Les Hyde

Booker Training Associates
Lexington, MO 64067
913.232.0244

www.bookertraining.com

Editor: Jackie Simmons

Table of Contents

Acknowledgments

Thanks to all those who helped me learn and grow in Leadership, Relationships, and Faith:

- My family, one & all, who taught me much
- My parents, who modeled 'leadership & relationship'
- Ron Black, a friend who led me to the Lord
- My wife Sydney, who is wonderful & led me closer to Him
- Military peers, commanders, & leadership experiences
- My children, Lesa and JD, now adults & leaders
- Stacy, John, Jackie, & Teresa
- Ed Butler; J. L., Fran & Greg,...great friends & leaders
- Students who have taught me much
- Jackie, who did so much as my Editor
- My church & pastors
- The 20 friends & professionals – characters in the book
- YOU, ...for your interest in leadership & self improvement

This is additionally dedicated to those being *managed* now;
that they may learn through these pages, understand their own mis-management
and become Great 8 Principled leaders themselves!

Introduction and Purpose

Our learning here is done by means of a story that will provoke plenty of thinking, ideas, and questions about leadership and management. Have you personally ever struggled with ineffective management—in yourself, your peers, or maybe your own boss? I think we all have at some point.

Debra, Les, and other characters in this story experience a scenario you will recognize and resemble. As you read this book, you will connect with your worlds of leadership, management, and teams as well as workplace relationships and culture.

This book is for leaders of all industries, businesses, and organizations. It is not intended exclusively for, or even focused on, corporate managers in particular. If you are interested in learning about leading others, you have found the right book. After reading this book, you will understand how real leadership works in small businesses, nonprofit organizations, families, churches, communities, large corporations, and anyplace that there are people who need to be led.

This book is about application and real people—it is not a fable or humorous story about some imaginary characters or critters. Our learning here involves people with real-life issues. You will recognize and connect with the folks you have come across in your own world.

We will share a story about leading, relationships, culture, flawed management thinking, human relations, individual and organizational behavior, teams, and so on. We will do so without lost mice, fish flying around, or penguins falling from icebergs! (Those were all great little stories, by the way.) It is not about leading in a minute or any other kind of short-lived program to make managing people instantly easy. It is about the realities of workplace management, providing answers and a lot of behavioral "how to," complete with **Return on Investment (ROI)** thinking. This is not just a warm and fuzzy approach to leading, but executable, up-close and behavioral *stuff* that really works. It is about bottom-line profits and productivity. We believe you will find the content here hits home and is closely aligned to your situation, your challenges, your boss, your behaviors, and your business, organization, or workplace.

Please note that this book is meant to be practical, applicable and useful. The size of the book will allow you to travel with this conference's learning material anywhere you go. There is room to make notes in the margins of most pages throughout the book in case you like to jot down your thoughts as you read. Also, please note that the sponsors, facilitators, staff members, and players throughout the conference (and book) are, for the most part, real people. Contact information is provided in case you want to contact any one of them in an appendix in the back of this book.

Please realize that the content presented during the conference, as well as the book, is only an overview. We have tried to provide key points and hit on the most important learning concepts but there is much more to learn. The 'Great 8 Leadership Principles' curriculum has been developed and the training and coaching experienced by the characters in these pages is ready and available for you or your organization to learn right now. Lastly there are subtle leadership issues and challenges throughout, outside of the actual conference and sessions. We encourage you to look for them and consider them as well in regard to your individual and organizational leadership development.

Our Story Begins

Debra stormed into Les's office. The routine of showing up in Les's office for coffee each morning has been going on for years now. However, the peaceful socializing that usually happens this time of day isn't going to happen today. Debra is visibly upset, in fact, she's livid! She frequently flies off the handle at the smallest of issues, so her emotional state isn't all that unusual. Her demeanor and presence suggests that she is a tad bit more upset than she is during one of her normal tirades, though, since this time she slammed the door shut behind her!

In honest moments with only her closest friends, Debra admits her divorce a year ago left her struggling more than ever with her temper. She is quick to go on the attack and this affects all of her relationships. Those she manages frequently suffer the brunt of her personal issues.

Les was staring out the window and looking across the parking lot while he was speaking on the phone to his son. Even so, he caught a glimpse of Debra coming through the door, and shoving the door behind her. As he spun around in his chair, Les grinned—when he did not receive a smile in return, he realized that he needed to end the call quickly, even though there were some important personal issues he needed to discuss with his son. Les knew just what Debra was angry about and he'd been dreading this encounter.

Les told his teenage son, Jackson, that he had to go and would touch base with him later, after school. Jackson was Les's only child, and he had raised him on his own up until two years ago. Jackson's mother, Les's first wife, had died in an accident when Jackson was just a baby.

Les was a single dad for about fifteen years before he married his current wife, Mickey, a couple of years ago. Mickey had been Les's high school flame many years back. She had reentered the picture when she and Les found each other again through an online dating site. Mickey and Jackson had some initial struggles, but things were great now between them; they were like a real mother and son. Les had done a decent job of raising Jackson, but teenagers could demand a lot of attention. Les and Mickey found themselves doing a lot of parenting these days.

Debra and Les discussed, on occasion, the similarities between workplace management and leadership at home. That wouldn't be part of their conversation today.

"This is crap, and you knew all about it, didn't you?" Debra began unloading as Les set the phone down. "The CEO is sending me to some stupid leadership conference and you were in on it, weren't you?" Barely taking a breath, she continued, "Being made to go! The CEO is not asking me if I want to go, not offering," Debra finally took a breath, "but directing me to go because he knows I damn sure wouldn't be going otherwise. Isn't that right?"

Les wheeled his chair around the desk, scooting with his feet and motioning for Debra to sit down in her usual spot. She declined and paced around instead. Les got up and moved to the door, opening it slightly. You know the chatter that goes on around here about us, anyway. All we need is to be in here behind closed doors. The gossip hounds will go to work; the rumor mill will be in full swing by noon. Let's not give them reason to talk about that big romance thing we got going on between us."

"Yeah, yeah, yeah—let 'em talk. None of them better bring any of that stuff up to me today, that's for sure. I might just make up and give them some juicy stuff to really talk about." Debra knew he was right, as rumors about them had made their way around the plant a couple of times over the last few years. Les and Debra enjoyed the hoopla, giving HR stress as they would provoke and 'mess with folks' about the issue.

Les was smirking as he stood and strolled back behind his desk and grabbed his coffee. "Yeah, I knew about it, but the CEO asked me to keep quiet about it until he could tell you himself after getting back from the LA trip. Guess you got the word?" He was halfway smiling, realizing she wouldn't think the comment was too funny.

Les continued without waiting for a response, "You do realize with me being CFO—the guy in charge of the bucks and the budget—that I did need to be part of this? Sorry I couldn't say anything sooner, buddy."

Debra continued to ignore another invitation to sit down, walked over and leaned against the file cabinet, and said, "I have been in management for fourteen or maybe fifteen years, leading people. I never needed any of that warm and fuzzy leadership stuff before and I don't need any now. It's a waste of time. I know how to manage! You, the CEO, and that knucklehead HR manager—you and your leadership development ideas! Give me a break. Look at the programs you guys have brought in over the last few years, those so-called leadership, change development, quality and motivational deals. Throwing fish around was a good concept, but what good was it? All we are left with are those stupid stuffed fish toys lying around on book shelves. Then those other programs and, oh, yeah, Team Building for Success, wow, now don't we have some awesome teams around here now because of that worthless training? What's come of any of those? What good did they do us? They are all just a waste of our money." Debra walked over to top off her mug of coffee, spilling a bit as she put the pot back. You could almost always count on coffee being available in Les's office.

Debra finally sat down. "I've met or exceeded production numbers routinely" she said, "and they've been over 90% in most every area this past year again. Plus, I'm the only one who's been under budget the last three quarters straight and customer service complaints are down. Need I go on? I venture to say that I know this company and this business as well as anyone around here outside of maybe, you, and well... no, probably *just* you, as a matter of fact!"

Les wheeled back around his desk while seated in one of the low-back seats that had been facing his desk. "Look, just relax" he said. "I know you don't buy into this stuff, but hear me out. This wasn't a total surprise. We have been talking about some development opportunities for you for a few months now. I am not going to get into all of it right now because I only have a couple of minutes. Besides, you *are* going. But how about this—I'm going with you!" Les smiled, hoping for some change in Debra's body language. There wasn't much, if any, just a subtle look of surprise revealed by her raised eyebrows.

As he walked over to top off his own cup, Les continued, "I told the CEO that I wanted to go and he cleared it. Just you and I, pal, and Mickey is going, too." He smiled, but he was certain it wouldn't be reciprocated. But then, Debra did smile just a bit, since she really liked Mickey.

"Look, this is a costly conference—some expensive stuff" he continued. "You must be important to the company, my friend, for us to spend that kind of money on you. Did you think of that?" Les nudged her, smiling, trying to get some hint of a grin, looking for an answer. He got nothing but a hard punch in the arm back.

Debra and Les were, indeed, close friends. They had a dotted-line reporting relationship—a dotted line from Debra to Les, who had a direct reporting line to the CEO. It was awkward at times, but they managed to make it work. This upcoming summer, Les would mark his twenty-year anniversary at TC, Incorporated. Les had been part of the interviewing team when Debra was hired seven years ago. The two had developed a close bond right away. Along with morning chats, they also socialized outside the office now and then. Debra and Mickey had connected as well; the three enjoyed going out and had dinner together a few times each month.

"Listen, I can only spare a couple of minutes" Les said, "since I have to get to the acquisition meeting and can't be late—there will be some important visitors in attendance. But, let me just share some quick thoughts with you here and then I'll see you over at Mulligan's after work tonight. Mickey will be there too, so I'll meet you both. Be prepared to listen to her go on about Mulligan's serving alcohol—I think she wants to bring back the days of Prohibition! It looks like I'm going to have to listen to both of your complaints."

Les went on as Debra nodded in agreement, her mood, posture, and facial expressions mellowing a bit. "Look, it's just me here, pal, and we've spoken about this plenty of times" Les continued. "We both know leadership is something you could use some help with. I don't need you to acknowledge that fact right now, while you're mad, but just listen to me for a minute. I believe in the difference real leadership can make. That 'warm and fuzzy' stuff as you like to put it—it's the stuff I try to practice with my folks. Anyway, I get to attend this two-day conference in *Kansas City*, and spend the evenings on a getaway with Mickey—I'm looking forward to that. There's nowhere better to be than in the Great Midwest in the springtime. We can all get away from this rainy, drizzly, so-called Seattle Rain Festival for a couple of days."

"Obviously, you're skeptical about how valuable leadership development conferences are," Les went on. "You are one of those managers who need convincing of its value, the Return on Investment (ROI). That's kind of an interesting twist on things, isn't it? You're the one worried about the value and expense involved in attending this conference, and I'm the CFO! Maybe there's a point there—since I am the CFO, maybe I have a better understanding of the ROI and that allows me to be more confident. Did you consider that?"

Les was smiling, waiting for her to concur. After Debra gave a slight nod, Les continued, "Listen, you and I are going with a mission, a very clear purpose. I want you to be open-minded yet determined to achieve our goal there. Here's the deal—I'm going because I know that I have more to learn and I value any learning and growth opportunities. What I want, and what the CEO wants as well, is for you to go and play the devil's advocate. We're going to roll out a sustainable leadership development process at this company sometime in the near future. We want to hit it really hard for the next couple of years, so we want to see if these people have what it takes to help us put our plan into action. In addition, we want to get some clarity on ROI. So, I'm going because I see it as a good opportunity and also because I want to get a better grip on ROI. I want you there to disprove it all. How about that? Is that fair enough?

On top of all that, you know how passionate the boss is regarding leadership and is pushing the whole Women in Leadership agenda. He has substantially increased the women we have in managerial roles around here and sincerely wants you to lead that charge. He would love to see you become active and become a player in the movement in our society these days. You are already good my friend, a little sharpening of the tool regarding some of this leadership stuff would make you one of the best managers I personally know of either gender.

Besides," Les continued, "look at the topics we're going to be learning about—I jotted down a few that caught my eye." Les pointed at the white board, where he had scribbled topics and dynamics before Debra had arrived that morning:

Relationships, (360) built on trust
'Real' Power Teams
Delegation / Project Management
Boss and Buddy
ROI – (absolutely)
Establishing Expectations
Micromanaging – Understanding It
Facilitating & Teaching
Accommodating People and Ideas
Depth in Communications

Creating Nonthreatening Environments

Consensus

Trust, Teams / even with Senior Managers

How we lie to people?

Fixing that Rumor Mill

<u>The Great 8:</u> Relate, Communicate, Evaluate, Eliminate, Create, Facilitate, Accommodate, Demonstrate

"Everything they are speaking about, the CEO and I want you to challenge—seek out the ROI and don't let up until you're sold" Les said. "I know you think you could never be convinced, but give it a chance. At the CEO's direction HR found this particular conference because it is marketed as addressing management skepticism and demonstrating ROI to the manager and organization. Additionally, the boss checked within his network of executives and got some good reports from them about this conference. Look, to your credit, you are assessing things from what they bring to the organization. You're asking what the value, return, and gain for the company is. I wish we had more managers with those concerns and priorities, to be honest with you."

Debra finally conceded, sat down next to Les, and replied, "Look, I know you've got to go. Let me process this information over the day today. I'm still pretty upset about how all of this transpired. On top of everything, it is especially untimely with the attention the new product launch needs—it's putting a lot of stress on me."

Les muttered, "Cool. We'll talk tonight. But it sounds like you're micromanaging that new product launch. You are well aware of how your folks complain about the way you micromanage projects on their quarterly surveys." Les was grinning ear to ear, and without giving Debra a chance to react, said, "Your launch will go fine. You shouldn't have any problem trusting your project manager with it, should you?"

Les knew that Debra got the point since this was an issue which the two of them had frequently discussed and argued about in the past. Her lack of trust, problem with delegating work, and inability to develop people she could trust, along with being a perfectionist—all of these inefficient work practices were holding her back, and they both knew it.

"Listen, Debra, you could really benefit from this conference. Now, I have to, and you have to also get out of here. Let's talk some more tonight and we'll strategize a bit more on the flight down to Kansas City. I've worked out all of your commitments with your assistant, Kendra. Dang, she's so efficient, by the way. You know, I need a new assistant—I ought to steal her from you!"

They both smiled, Debra for the first time that morning, since they both knew that wouldn't really happen. "Anyway, Kendra has your calendar cleared" Les continued. "The boss, the chief operating officer, and I are indeed well aware of the importance of the new product launch but, unlike you, we trust Jack to get the briefs ready and to stay after it through completion. You can badger him all you want over the phone while we're there, you ol' badger, you!" he said, taking another shot at her.

"I have to go. I'll see you tonight at Mulligan's. One more thing—I know you and how you tend to take things out on your people. Try to be conscious of that today and don't let your attitude about all this affect your management—oh, that would be more like *leadership*, wouldn't it? Give your people a break, they didn't do anything. This conference isn't their fault!"

Les was grabbing folders and his planner from his credenza while he refilled his coffee and smiled smugly. He was moving fast now. He had taken some serious shots at her leadership abilities. Debra and Les were close, tight, and he knew she could handle it. They challenged and messed with each other all the time and their friendship always endured no matter how tense things got between them.

Les was responsible for much of what Debra knew about leadership. She had come a long way in the years since she'd been hired at TBI. Debra was downright brutal with people when she started at the company. She knew that the discussions she had with Les, whom she respected as a leader, had helped her.

As he started to walk out the door, Les stopped briefly, leaned against the door frame, and said, "You think you've got problems. Ana is back to his old ways—his grades are down and he failed an Algebra test last Friday. He's worried that he might not get to run in the state track meet at the end of the month. It's his own fault, but he's definitely bummed and I guess I am, too. Managing people at work and leading a family at home—both require similar skills. Maybe we both need some help from this conference; you need help with workplace management and I need to learn more about parenting leadership! Hopefully, we'll both find some nuggets there. See you at Mulligan's. Have a great day. As always, remember, it doesn't get any better than this!"

Debra stared out the window and then plopped into Les's desk chair for a while. This situation was seriously impacting her self-esteem and confidence. She began to doubt her management skills. What else did she have in life if not her job, her profession? Now even that was in doubt it seemed. What if she failed at that, as well? Debra got up, walked around, and then sat back down at Les's desk again. She found a notepad and decided to try to capture some of her thoughts. Debra had gotten into the habit, recently, of keeping a journal, so she wrote a few things down.

Met with Les, his office—being sent to training

My management weaknesses?

What if I was better at leading?

What would it mean to the bottom line, ROI?

How is my team, really?

Trust: Is it okay to go away and trust them to get it done?

Right now, what leadership means to me is:

>directing, being clear, holding people accountable
>
>being available and willing to work with people
>
>being supportive, sharing what I know,
>
>solving problems decisively

Training in leadership seems to be a waste to me, anyway.

This conference will be more of the same. I will go with a positive approach and prove my point!

Oh, yeah, another leadership thing: being open-minded...

...I'm not bad right now, I know – always room for improvement!

Just then, Debra remembered that her sister was coming for a visit at the end of the month. Debra had a terrible relationship with her. That's just dandy, she thought. That will be right after we return from the conference. Her sister was jobless, nearly broke, and needed to be with someone, and unfortunately that someone was going to be Debra. What timing.

Debra quickly thought of God, and that she needed Him. After a brief prayer, she thought some more and jotted down some notes. Afterward, she got up and shut Les's door. She needed some more time to think before the day began.

Debra's divorce—her second—had really hurt and damaged her. She was shattered when her ex suddenly left one day, for reasons only a few people knew about. Les and Mickey knew that Debra was partially responsible for the problems in the marriage, but no one thought that Debra deserved to be deserted. Mickey and Les had nursed Debra through the initial days after that. Debra even stayed at their home for a few nights.

As Les was walking over to Mulligan's he did some thinking. He could empathize with Debra's situation since his parents had divorced when he was eleven years old, and he remembered the turmoil the entire family went through. Les's father had disappeared from the family after the divorce, and Les never saw him after that; he was raised by his mom, who received some help from his grandparents.

Les thought about the number of people he knew who either admitted to having a dysfunctional family or talked about someone they knew who did. Conflict seemed to be more prevalent these days, he thought, especially in the workplace. He pondered the impact of this increase in employees dealing with the stress that came from dealing with family problems. The breakdown in families and of society, he thought managing people was even more of a challenge, more than ever.

Les often preached to the managers and supervisors he led about the dynamics and challenges leaders faced. He often said that it was amazing that anything resembling teamwork was possible. No wonder there was conflict, when people were dealing with problems at home such as ineffective parenting, divorce, abuse, and misunderstandings due to poor communication. To make matters worse, so many managers, including Les, came from those same environments and traumatic experiences. Yikes!

At Mulligan's That Night

Mickey and Les were at a table far from the juke box—the quietest spot in the place. Debra came through the side entrance, followed by a few others who rushed in as they tried to get out of the rain. This particular storm was stronger than most in the northwest—it was not only raining, but hard, and the wind was howling.

"I ordered you a light beer from the tap—hope that's okay" Les told Debra as she approached the table. "I told the waitress you needed a tall one fast!" Les leaned back and waited for Debra to pick up where she'd left off when their morning's rather heated conversation had abruptly ended. He was shocked to see that Debra was much calmer and he was *very* surprised to hear that she was not only ready but actually looking forward to the challenge the trip presented.

Before he had a chance to consider Debra's new attitude, Mickey leaned forward and said, "So, you two, why are we meeting here? You both know I don't appreciate the bar scene. You know how the Bible views this sort of thing and it's just wrong. You're leaders, you should know better! I just hope nobody from church is here. How can you say you are Christians and then go on drinking? Les, I know you're tired of hearing this from me, but I'm not letting up anytime soon. It's a good thing I love you—yeah, and you, too, Debra. Well, I guess I've had my say for the moment. Debra, how was your day?"

Debra was a bit offended to just ignore what Mickey had said to just go on about her day. The three friends, not for the first time, hammered around their views about alcohol. Mickey thinks that the Bible clearly states that drinking alcohol is wrong, a sin; Debra and Les do not agree. Debra takes great pride in her relationship with Jesus but thinks the Word says no such thing. Les muttered a sarcastic comment about not caring if someone from the church did show up. Les loved debating about the different ways of interpreting the Bible while Mickey, on the other hand, thought that everything was clearly stated as it was and not subject to interpretation.

Les cut things off before the conversation got too heated, saying, "I told you, Debra. I told you that we shouldn't meet here." Les, wearing an impish grin on his face, paused a moment and said, "I really didn't tell her that, Mickey. It's just that this place is cool and convenient. We are all flawed in different ways and you know that I just don't think that drinking alcohol is sinning against God. I've had enough of this argument for the time being. Please, let's hold off on this discussion, Honey, and we'll talk about it some more soon, I promise."

Everyone was quiet for a brief, awkward moment until Les spoke up and said, "Mickey, it would probably interest you to know that this is actually an issue that our company's management is looking into right now. At the past few executive meetings, the topic of leaders and employees socializing with each other has been on the agenda. I know what I think about drinking alcohol or any other form of recreation after hours with those you lead; I also know that Debra has a different opinion than I do. Maybe we'll pick up some ideas at the conference."

As he finished speaking, Les leaned over and kissed Mickey on the cheek and continued, "Now, on another note, and to change the subject," Les smiled at Mickey and then turned to Debra, "tell me, what's up with the new attitude, Deb?"

Debra paused, took a sip of beer as she looked at Mickey and then back to Les and said calmly, "A fricking micromanager, you say! That's what you think I am? Maybe so, but maybe that's why I get such good numbers in most areas. You can't argue with results, can you?"

"Yeah, well in most areas" Les said aggressively. "What about your turnover numbers? Those are always higher than the norm."

As Debra's face flushed, Les continued, "Okay, okay, Deb. Wait, a moment. Mickey and I were just talking about the issue we're having with Ana—the one I mentioned to you this morning. I know it seems like I'm getting away from the subject at hand here, but bear with me." Les turned to Mickey and continued in a frustrated tone, "Dang it, you know I thought he had his grades under control and was making them a priority. His grades improved for a whole semester, then at Christmas we caved in and bought him the puppy we'd promised him if he…"

Mickey broke in, "You know, as much as I really like that little dog, I wish we hadn't done it. Should I be thinking that way? He's such a pain in the butt, anyway—the dog, I mean, not Jackson. Well, then again, I guess they both are!"

They all chuckled as Mickey continued, "Anyway, that dog is just like having another kid, but to tell you the truth, I wouldn't get rid of Chief for anything now. That mutt has grown on all of us hasn't he, Les? And now our neighbors down the street, the Allison's, are going to have to babysit, I mean dog-sit that dog as well as watch Jackson when we go to Kansas City. They say they don't mind, but still…"

Les retorted, "I talked to Doc Allison and they are really okay with the situation, especially since they can always just stick the dog in our back yard now and then. Since Doc's a veterinarian anyway, they always have one stray or another around visiting them—I really figure they don't much care.

The possibility of Ana missing the state track meet is a drag. I really think that the coaches are just letting him sweat it out until they see some improvement in his performance. They will probably let him run as long as he earns a better score on the makeup exam, and I think he'll do that. The coaches are messing with Ana in order to teach him about accountability. Sounds like leadership stuff, huh, Deb?" Les asked.

Debra, wiping condensation from her mug as she listened, offered some words of encouragement. "All that will work out" she said. "He's a great kid. Sure, the coaches are going to mess with him. The question is what the parents should do. Les, maybe you'll learn some parenting leadership tips at the conference. Maybe you need to take the trip and learn about leadership more than I do."

Debra gave Les a light slap on the back. He and Mickey agreed that there was always more to learn about parenting. Then Les said, "Of course, you still have a thing or two to learn about curtailing employee turnover."

Debra didn't appreciate the jab, but she decided not to dignify it with a response. She said, "Okay. We don't need to go there. I'm not arguing. I'm prepared to give this thing a try if, for no other reason, than to have the satisfaction of proving you and the CEO wrong. I'll take plenty of notes regarding ROI. You can count on that being my main focus. I don't care how they're presenting and marketing this conference, I know it will probably be a lot of trust-building exercises, team rah-rah stuff, and even some group hugging. I'm telling you now, I'm sincerely going in open-minded, but I'll still be after justification and proof. I will be their biggest critic, but I promise to be tactful about it. Fair enough? Well then, let's say we get some menus and order something to eat."

Les hoisted his drink up for a toast and replied, "Good idea. It's definitely time to eat and you've got the mindset that the CEO and I are looking for. I thought that our time here tonight was going to be a drag—that I'd have to listen to you whine about going—but I'm glad to be proven wrong this time. Now we can have some good pub food and enjoy the evening. Maybe we should take the kid and the dog, after all, since it's the home of the Chiefs, Ana's favorite football team—nah, I reckon not. That would make the trip too chaotic. But listen, I don't know how much you've looked at the program, but..."

"Actually," Debra interrupted, "I glanced at it and put it in the shredder" she confessed, sheepishly. "My immediate reaction was that there was no way that I was going to go, so I wouldn't need it. Do you have another copy?"

Les slapped the table as he laughed, "I can't believe it! Never mind—yes I can! Yes, I'll make you a copy and you can pick it up when you come in for coffee in the morning. I registered you already, but there is one part of the program you need to respond to. On Saturday night, there is a dinner and the theme is, "God Knows Leadership." It's being held across the street in the new Power & Light entertainment district at a host restaurant. The lecture and discussion will be about bringing God into the workplace and being mindful of Him when making leadership decisions. At first I thought I'd skip it, since I'm a good Catholic and I can't imagine how I could put that sort of information to use, but you know Mickey—there's no way she's going to let us pass on it! So, we're going. You need to let them know if you're going to attend, too. Assuming you are going, when you do, ask to be seated with me and Mickey."

Debra smiled excitedly and high-fived Mickey. "Well, you know me" she said. "I am definitely in on that! Thank the Lord. Something beneficial might come out of this weekend after all—learning how to include God in the workplace! That definitely intrigues me, since I'm never sure about how much I should talk about being a Christian without being labeled a Jesus freak by nonbelievers. Who's the speaker?"

Friday, the Flight There

Les, Mickey, and Debra were driving to Sea-Tac Airport after an early morning executive staff meeting. They had to make a 9 o'clock flight but they were making good time. It was only 8 o'clock and they were almost there. It was misty and a bit chilly outside. Les tossed a program to Debra, who was sitting in the back seat, and said, "You can look at an original since you shredded yours." He laughed and nudged Mickey. The flight was uneventful. Once they landed at Kansas City International Airport, however, Les received a text message from Jackson. It read:

CHIEF HIT BY CAR N DRIVEWAY.
WISH U WERE HERE.
CALL WHEN U CAN.

Les called Jackson back right away. Jackson told him that Chief had snuck out the back door and was loose when the Allison's son backed the car out of the driveway and ran him over. Chief was nearly killed. Jackson was sure he would die and was badly shaken. Fortunately Doc, being a veterinarian, was right there and able to give Chief the care he needed immediately. It turned out that Chief suffered from a broken back leg and some bruising and he was in a lot of pain until Doc gave him some medication to calm him down and take the edge off. Jackson handed the phone over to Doc, who told Les that both Jackson and the dog would be alright, and that Jackson was probably more upset than Chief was at the moment. Doc promised to keep Les and Mickey posted, and apologized, over and over, for what had happened.

While Les and Mickey were occupied on the phone, Debra took a moment to look at the agenda from the program Les had given to her.

The Great Eight Conference for Leaders
Sprint Center • Kansas City

Day One: Saturday

Networking, Breakfast	7:30 am
Opening Session	8:30 am
Breakout Session #1	9:30 am
Breakout Session #2	11:00 am
Lunch	12:30 pm
Breakout Session #3	1:30 pm
Breakout Session #4	3:00 pm
Evening Social (Optional)	6:30 pm

Day Two: Sunday

Church Service (Optional)	6:30 am
Breakout Session #5	8:00 am
Brunch	9:30 am
Breakout Session #6	10:00 am
Breakout Session #7	11:30 pm
Snack	1:00 pm
Breakout Session #8	2:00 pm
Wrap-Up Session	4:00 pm

COMMUNICATE • **RELATE** • EVALUATE • **CREATE**
ELIMINATE • FACILITATE • **ACCOMMODATE** • DEMONSTRATE

Opening Meeting of Conference

Les found three seats about a third of the way back from the front row. The room was a plush, moderately-sized auditorium, just at the east end of the Sprint Center. There were a few other events taking place in the facility and there had been a big concert the night before. The Great Eight Conference for Leaders had an entire wing to themselves. There were posters advertising a concert for a Beatles-copy, look-alike band on Monday night, and Mickey and Les were thinking about staying over another night so they could go to it.

Meanwhile, Mickey was getting signed up for a day trip for spouses, which included touring historic homes, antiquing, lunch, and a visit to the Civil War battle field. She also learned about the 150th anniversary of the famous Battle of Lexington, in 2011.

John Landsberg, a local KC businessman and friend was assisting Mickey and others with the trip coordination. John was a sponsor, helped with PR aspects and some content areas; and was an old friend of Booker's when both were faculty at a local university.

Mickey knew Les was going to be getting antsy and grabbed a card of John's heading quickly toward the Opening session.

Mickey would be taking the 40-minute bus ride from Kansas City to Lexington at 9:30, after the Opening Session. As she strolled over to the presentation room to meet up with Les and Debra, Mickey mused to herself that Lexington seemed to be a nice bedroom community. Lexington attracted retirees and people who worked in Kansas City who wanted to live in a small town.

Les was keeping an eye out for Mickey and Debra as he looked over the crowd. He guessed there had to be between 125 and 150 people present. Les had expected many more. He discovered later that the Great Eight Conference for Leaders maintained a strict facilitator to participant ratio. Small-group learning was an important aspect of their instructional method and they normally did three separate two-day conferences in each city they visited.

Les stirred impatiently. Debra had excused herself on the way in, and he looked around, trying to locate her. He figured she was just calling in to work in order to micromanage some more, and chuckled to himself. Just then, Les noticed that his phone was vibrating. Jackson was calling. Les decided that the call would have to wait, since the opening session was about to begin. He didn't want to miss a single word of the presentation.

"Welcome, welcome, welcome!" an attractive lady shouted into the microphone, waving at the crowd as she paced along the center of the stage. Her name was Judy Neu from KC and she was one of the breakout facilitators; she would soon become one of Les and Debra's favorites.

Judy quickly and capably gained the audience's attention; they became quiet and focused on what she had to say. She was making some administrative announcements when Debra and Mickey showed up, clumsily scooting in front of Les's knees to the seats he had saved for them.

There was a PowerPoint presentation running behind Judy; the slides had been running on a continuous loop for the last fifteen minutes or so. Sponsors and upcoming conventions were advertised. The Great Eight Conference for Leaders would soon travel to Albuquerque, San Francisco, Atlanta, Washington DC, Chicago, San Antonio, a few locations in Canada, and even Australia. Everyone seemed impressed with how big and global the conference was.

Information was given about books, CDs, curriculum, and other materials that would be available in the foyer over the next two days. Les was excited to learn that some players for some of the local sports teams would stop by the conference during the breaks. Booker, the conference host, was a huge Royals fan, so there were for sure a few Royals players would be visiting. Les discovered that he and Booker had the same favorite player in common. They had both followed Amos Otis, an All-Star outfielder for the team throughout the 1970s, since they were kids. The Royals, the Chiefs, and the local pro soccer team were all represented as well as the area's three largest universities—Kansas University (KU), Kansas State, and Missouri University (MU). Additional announcements and sales pitches were made about contacting the Great Eight Conference to schedule training sessions at individual towns, businesses, churches, and so on.

Judy spoke loudly, "Greetings! I am Judy, I am a Training and Development Professional and as my business motto says, *Maximizing Human Potential*—that's precisely what all this is about as well. I will be seeing all of you later during our sessions. Welcome to each of you. For now, I want to quickly introduce you to our host and pass you along to him. He likes to be called Booker, and he is coming up here now to share some opening thoughts with you. His is our founder and overall conference leader, the author of three books, and he has been working in the organizational leadership field for nearly two decades. He is the president of the Great Eight Conference for Leaders. Prior to his organizational leadership career, he had a distinguished career as a military officer. You know, I was just thinking, that must make him pretty old, doesn't it?"

The audience laughed as Judy and Booker gestured toward each other. Judy quickly continued, "Just kidding, boss—sort of!" Then Judy put the back of her hand to the side of her mouth and mock-whispered to the audience, "If I build him up a bit more here, he'll forget all about that comment!"

Booker had put this whole routine together, drawing on concepts from his books and enacting them for the crowd. Judy told the audience that Booker's first two books of the Leadership Conversation series were available for purchase in the lobby. The third book, which much of this conference was based on, would be given to participants before they left—the cost was included in their registration fee for the conference.

A smattering of applause followed. Judy gestured dramatically, as if she were a game-show host, toward Booker and said, "So, enough of all this.

Oh, my, he's going to have such a big head! Let's get on with things. Here's your host, our fearless leader, a former professor of mine in graduate school, my friend and soon to be your friend, too, Booker!"

Booker swept Judy into a brief hug as he walked onto the stage, then continued on to the front and center edge. He was quite close to the front rows. "Well, hey, does it get any better than this?" he asked. "Here we are in the Great Midwest, in beautiful sunny Kansas City, 75 degree weather, basking in the spring sunshine while we learn—wow. It would be a great day for some golf, huh? You probably don't know this, but I grew up around here, in a little town off of I-70 to the east called Lexington. Anyway, we are so glad you are here and home that you will find these two days to be immensely valuable. I hope you are up for a challenge and to be challenged in your thinking!" People in the audience reacted positively. Debra was sitting quietly with a stoic expression on her face. She rolled her eyes periodically, and prepared herself for what she was sure would wind up being a big waste of time.

"Quickly, here's some food for thought. Let me ask you: What's your attitude as you sit here right now? Think about it. Are you positive, negative, excited, upset, impatient, not really buying it, resistant, or what?" Booker paused, looking around and giving the audience a few moments to consider the questions. Some people raised their hands, others shouted out some positive exclamations, and there was a smattering of applause.

He continued, "Listen, we realize that most of you are here voluntarily but that some of you are not. Some were more or less sent by their employers, right? Can you believe that—someone being forced to go to training? Now you, being the leader that you are, each of you, you would surely never do such a thing to the people you manage! No one here has ever forced change or sent someone to something they didn't ask for!

Nah! So, if you were one of the people whose manager directed them to be here, maybe you have a negative attitude about this conference. I think we have a leadership lesson here. Managers force change and cram it down people's throats without asking for their opinions; leaders don't do it his way. See, we're already learning something! When people are squirming, becoming aware, feeling a little guilt or discomfort, I think that's the first step to real learning."

Les subtly elbowed Debra, cleared his throat, and smiled without looking at her. Debra grimaced back at him and muttered that he was one of those leaders who force change.

Booker paused deliberately, and then strolled across to the far side of the stage. Some people chattered quietly, laughed, and pointed at their companions. "Here's the deal," Booker continued, "We know that's the case for some of you. If I'm talking about you, then, since you're here anyway, try to get what you can out of it. Be your old skeptical self—that's cool. In fact, we insist that you look at us critically and skeptically. We realize that some of you are here to prove that leadership development training doesn't work. We want you to try, sincerely, to prove that to yourself. We urge you to attempt to disprove the value of leadership training during your time here and within each of the breakout sessions. On the flip side, you also need to agree to go about this training with an open mind—you need to be willing to take both sides into consideration. But please know that your tactful challenges to our facilitators are welcome. We want to prove ROI, or Return on Investment, to you." Booker paused again, and smiled.

"So, what are we doing here, anyway?" Booker asked. "Let me take a few minutes to give you some introductory thoughts to get your 'thinker' thinking. Please understand, especially you skeptics out there, that we realize that one day or even two days of training doesn't turn someone into a leader—even at this awesome Great Eight Conference. Still, we're confident that you'll bring a lot back with you to build on and work on."

"As you can see," Booker continued, "our agenda focuses on eight principles. We have studied leadership behavior in lots and lots of leaders over the years. Our conclusions are expressed in what we now call 'The Great Eight Leadership Principles. We know that we have something special here that can really help individual leaders and contribute to the organizational leadership field of knowledge, as well. We look forward to your critiques at the end of the sessions, so please take notes for yourself and to share with us. We really look forward to sharing with you, as well as learning from each and every one of you. This is a professionally facilitated look at leadership concepts, and the eight principles are designed to provide a framework for anyone who leads. We're going to present a guide for managing people in an effective and productive manner. We believe that understanding these eight concepts will make any leader more effective and well-rounded. By practicing these principles, you will be better able to take care of people so that they can help you build your business. We will give you much more detail in the small breakout groups. We are not here to reiterate what you've already heard elsewhere or to throw a lot of definitions at you. We're going to give you the practical and strategic tools you need to apply to real-world situations. This is the stuff that really works! Let me show them to you briefly now, and then you'll go over each one in the breakout groups."

Booker paused, took a sip of water, and showed each slide and read them aloud slowly, giving the participants plenty of time to take in the information.

During the scrolling, Booker shared about how during the developmental stages of the Great 8, the term *APPLICATE* was bantered around a bit. The conference and curriculum developers wanted at one point to call the Great 8, *APPLICATION LEADERSHIP*. With the current focus and emphasis in our society and business world on *Apps* with smart phones, laptops, etc, the Great 8 Principles fit in perfectly. Booker stressed that all that would be shared over the two days was indeed about application; he also mentioned how they were developing an *App* currently to be made available to business professionals later this year.

Communicate

- Visioning
- Chain of Command
- Upward Flow
- Teach and Educate
- YOUR Wisdom
- Absolutes and Values

Relate

- 360 Degrees
- Socializing
- The HEART First
- Boss and Buddy
- 24 x 7
- Trust Barriers

Evaluate

- Self FIRST
- Mentor and Coach
- TEAM Competencies
- Fix versus Fire
- Annual Drill Gone
- ETA "Everywhere"

Create

- Culture of TEAM
- Systems and Processes
- TRUST, Again and Still
- CHANGE Mindset
- Challenge the WAYS
- No MAINTAINING

Eliminate

- Bottlenecks / Conflicts
- Rumor Mindset
- Threatening Environments
- Bad Apple Acceptance
- Criticism as a Bad Thing

Facilitate

- Consensus in ALL
- Continued Improvement
- Your PEOPLE System
- Teaching Fishing
- Grow Individual and TEAM
- 100% versus Anything Less

Accommodate

- Available to ALL
- Protect / Shield
- Do NOT Enable
- Time Management
- New Ideas and Thoughts
- Everyone Always

Demonstrate

- Model and Example
- Teaching and Learning
- Respect of Values
- The VISION
- Relationships!!!
- Professionalism
- Okay to be Wrong

"We believe that effective, caring leaders create an environment of success that attracts and retains the best talent" Booker said. "It eliminates waste, guides, educates, and puts the focus on achieving business goals that are aligned with personal goals as well as organizational growth and development. That's a mouthful, huh?"

"I know you skeptics might still be thinking that this won't help you meet your performance metrics or organizational challenges. Well, stay open-minded. Please consider, as a leader, how much tactical work you are doing. How much do you do right now at your workplace? It's likely that you don't do much, unless you micromanage your staff. There aren't any micromanagers out there, are there?" Debra shifted in her seat as Les smirked at her while Booker continued, "My guess is that you are in charge of a group of people who have tasks to accomplish. You direct, inform, delegate, and inspect to ensure that the work is done correctly, on time, and within budget. Listen, we make no bones about it—businesses exist to make money for the shareholders, and it takes people to run a business. If the business isn't producing the desired results, corrective changes need to be made. In order to meet shareholder demands, many leaders will make knee-jerk decisions and attempt unsustainable programs. These approaches are, unfortunately, prevalent in the workplace and frequently result in low morale, discipline issues, negative attitudes, poor attendance, excessive sick time, and high staff turnover."

"Picture this," Booker said, "maybe even close your eyes for a moment. No, really, go ahead and close them. We all know of at least one amazing, charismatic, seemingly natural leader. Do you know such a leader? Yes, that one. Picture them for a moment. Are you one of those one-of-a-kind leaders who make their jobs look easy? Could you become one? Yes, it's possible. If you learn and internalize what you'll be taught at this conference, the natural leader in you will awaken. But, let's not kid ourselves—that won't happen just because you've heard some stuff here over the weekend. So, let's also agree that while the opportunity to learn and develop will be given to you here, it's up to you to decide if you want to use what you've learned and make the effort to become a great leader."

"Leadership can be learned!" Booker continued. "It's obvious that we believe that, and that you do, too—the fact that you're here is proof of that. Well, unless you're one of those people who were sent here under duress!"

"Anyway, becoming an awesome leader requires further mentoring and reinforcement as well as continual feedback loops and coaching back at the ranch. Real behavioral learning doesn't happen through a workshop. It doesn't happen overnight, either, that's for sure. It requires a systematic approach of endless leadership development from the top down—and also sideways, from the bottom up—with continual reinforcement. We never get there—there are no perfect leaders. If you think you've achieved perfection as a leader, that's a sure sign that you're in big trouble! Why? Because if you believe you have nothing to learn, you stop learning and growing. You're done."

"Another thought is that it is far more likely that the ideal leader, the one you envisioned a few moments ago, did not possess their skill set naturally, from birth, straight from the womb! It's far more likely that those skills, qualities, characteristics, and behaviors were learned. Behaviors are learned through life experiences, usually from parents, teachers, preachers, coaches, bosses, and managers at different points in their lives. Now, if you want to argue with me about that, you can catch up with me another time, but better yet, here's an idea..." Booker paused, grinned largely, and pointed toward the lobby, "Go get my first book that's for sale in the lobby. Actually, my first *two* books address this idea in depth and thoroughly defend my argument. There is someone out there who will gladly sell you one or both," he continued, smiling and gesturing as he walked over to the podium.

"For our purposes here, we'll tell you how to take those skills, qualities, characteristics, and behaviors, and show you how to use them to become a real leader. That is, unless you believe that you already are one!" Booker's sarcastic tone was noted by the audience and he paused, observed their reactions, and then continued. "We know from plenty of solid research that 85 to 90 percent of those seemingly natural, awesome, charismatic leaders actually *learned* those skills somewhere along their life's journey—and you can, too."

"If you buy into the content here about what real behavioral, caring leadership truly means," he continued, "the possibilities are endless. If you are also willing to seek out trusted individuals to hold you accountable to your behavioral transformation, you, too, can transform yourself into a so-called natural leader. Indeed, if you learn how, then soon people will be looking at you and believe that *you* are a natural-born leader!"

"The fact that you are here right now—unless, as I said, you were coerced into coming here—says to me that you are, indeed, ready and want to become an effective, high-producing leader. Now, you must promise that once you become one, you will share what you've learned with others. This is an important issue that I really want you to think about. Leaders often learn new management and leadership skills and then keep them to themselves. Please don't do that. Continue to learn. Continue to teach. Whatever you take away from here, take it back, share it, and get others involved in making you, and them, better. Make sense?"

"Let me say that all again!" Booker said, enthusiastically. "We will give you all the materials, and a lot of ideas for you to think critically about. Take that back with you, process it, and discuss it with those you lead. Involve others, and you will all improve. By going over the ideas, teaching and preaching them, you are also reinforcing what you've learned and helping yourself to internalize the information. You have to promise now, okay?"

Let me share what we are intending to do over the next couple of days. Actually, our purpose should be clear to you now, so let me mention a few things that this conference is *not* about. First, let me assure you right now that this conference is not just a warm and fuzzy look at taking care of people. It's not about token efforts—stuff like managers smiling, group hugs, and morning rounds of saying hello. It's not about telling jokes, letting folks get away with stuff, giving employees meaningless incentive gifts, or pizza parties. Indeed, taking care of your people is about doing what is right as a leader—doing your job well. It is that job that most organizations never really teach clearly or effectively to their managers and supervisors. We want to focus on your behaviors, attitude, understanding, practices, and skills in leading your most valuable resources—your people."

"Let me also hit on another point. Return on Investment (ROI) is what business people focus on when discussing an investment, as well they should. When an investment is a fixed asset such as equipment or software, a business case might be developed, identifying the risks and rewards of the purchase. The decision-makers either agree the ROI makes sense and support the investment or they do not agree that it is worth the scarce resources available. Some of you are here to get a better understanding of leadership development and ROI. Please make sure you understand what you're taught about these topics and ask questions if you don't. We know that if you don't accept that this conference represents a good ROI, you won't accept anything else that you're taught here."

Booker turned to face the projection screen at the back of the stage and clicked the remote control. "We use this all the time as we work with managers when we're thinking about leadership and development, although I admit I'm unsure of the origin of this Q & A."

Management's Training Dilemma

Q: What if I train my people and they leave?
A: What if you don't and they stay?!

How does this apply to developing
leaders and leadership?

Lots of the participants pointed and chuckled and started talking amongst themselves. Booker refocused the audience and said, "It's an interesting thought, isn't it? When you present the investment as developing people—

of maximizing your available human capital—then the ROI is measured in a more accurate way. We know that leaders who learn and develop themselves produce a solid ROI, and we can back our claim with plenty of research—just ask if you'd like to see the data. The ROI is measurable, and you will learn how to measure it over the next two days. Let me also assure you that your organization probably has all the tools to measure it at its disposal already—after all, you're asked to measure everything else, aren't you?"

Booker went on, "Let me share another concept with you that we call CEO. I'm not talking about the Chief Executive Officer, either. Effective leaders need to care about and balance the needs of multiple stakeholders. They are interested in the organization and in doing what is best for everyone involved. You might ask yourself why you need to care for people other than the staff you're responsible for. Well, there are typically three separate entities that a leader and the organization need to be aware of in order to lead successfully and develop their teams to reach their potential and achieve high results." Booker clicked the remote and showed the CEO slide.

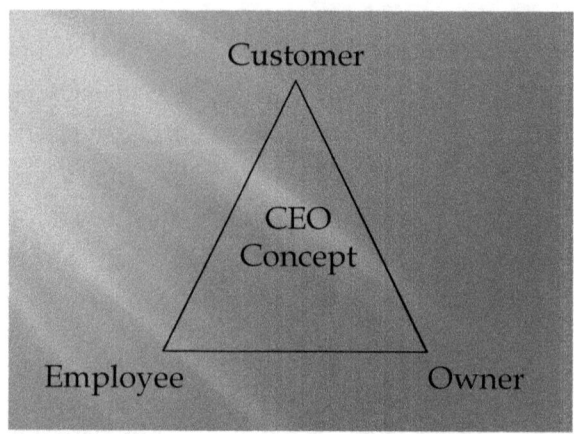

"As you can see, CEO stands for Customer, Employee, and Owner, which need to establish a symbiotic relationship if the business entity is to survive. You realize," Booker continued, "that if you take away one of these entities, the other two cannot survive. Leaders need to understand the needs of each respective entity, then educate their team on how to achieve the business results they're after. You will hear more about this during the breakout sessions. Maybe you've already gotten the point. This conference is about creating real leaders, and that includes you. It is about defining what leadership means and how a manager, supervisor, or executive leads people effectively. This is about the practices, principles, habits, actions, expectations, skills, understanding, and behaviors that result in you becoming a model caring leader. Again, group hugs and trust-falls are not the answer. Real caring leadership involves holding folks accountable in achieving the business metrics, needs and objectives.

As I prepare to wrap up here, let me ask you to go into your packet of materials and find a slip of paper titled, "Gimmicks and Programs." Grab it and peruse it for a moment, please. Check out this list of some of the popular management fads, programs, suggested practices, concepts, and gimmicks. This is what management has been sold as being the keys to effective leadership. Let me assure you, on behalf of those who have tried to utilize them that they do not work. I suspect that you recognize at least some of these."

Gimmicks and Programs are Not Leadership!

Administrative assistant sends birthday notes

Saying "good morning" to everyone at 8am

Workshops and seminars

Asking opinions when you don't care about the answers

Holiday turkeys

Incentive gifts such as tee-shirts, key chains, and coffee cups

Eating lunch with the President

Skip level meetings

MBWA

Motivational programs

Core value and mission exercises

Town Hall meetings

Annual picnics and pizza parties

Perfect attendance and employee of the month awards

Pay for performance

Spirit, Diversity, and Empowerment weeks

Surveys and assessments

You be the Boss days

Recognition parking spots

Promises of better benefits

*??? **Others you have seen** ???*

"Let me also be clear that nothing on this list is there because it is a bad thing on its own merit. Actually, these are all pretty good practices. In fact, putting them all into practice would make for an awesome place of work, but only if they were executed and led by knowledgeable, effective leaders. To some degree, we show you this list because we want you to know that we are not here to sell you on gimmicks or short-term programs. The Great Eight is not a "be all / end all" answer. It's pretty good stuff, mind you, but leadership is a never-ending learning and growing process. A leader needs to continue transforming, changing, and improving themselves."

"Again, there is nothing wrong with doing any of the aforementioned things, but simply doing any of them does not make a person a leader. I suspect that these gimmicks were invented by someone who lacked real leadership abilities. Certainly, a leader isn't made by just completing the tasks listed on their daily planner or carelessly doing whatever their administrative assistant reminds them to do. Being a leader is a way of life, an aspect of one's personality, a style. It's a way of working together with the people you lead and practicing the concepts you'll learn here in order to create a culture of leadership."

"These individual concepts and ideas on your list are the fodder for shows like *The Office* and inspire cartoons like *Dilbert*. That is because it is cartoonish to think that some manager with little or no understanding of what leadership is can just fall back on gimmicks without the people around them seeing the shallowness of their actions. It's a joke to believe that the people around you will think that you're a great leader because you gave them a gift or asked, insincerely, about their family. Come on now, would that work on you? Of course not, because you've already been in those shoes. You've seen these ploys attempted, and they never fooled you either I am guessing."

"There is much more to consider, and I hope that by the end of the weekend you have a thorough understanding of everything that's presented to you. Okay, we're done here for now. However, before you leave here and go on to your first breakout session, and since we're speaking of gimmickry," Booker paused and looked toward the projection screen behind him, "take a look at this box that I am putting up on the screen. I'll only show it to you for a moment. It's a box with a hole in it. Quickly examine the picture and decide which surface the hole is in."

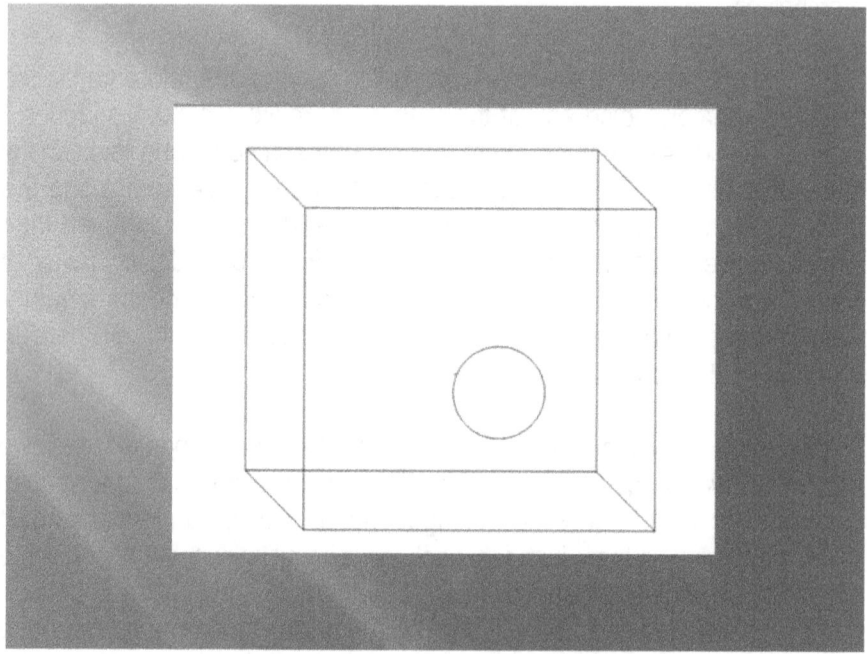

Booker allowed the participants a few seconds to view the slide, then clicked to a blank screen. "So, where did you see the hole?" he asked.

"How many think the hole is in the front of the cube, in the lower right-hand corner?" he asked, and several hands were raised. "How many think it's in the front of the cube, somewhere towards the center?" he asked and other hands were raised. "How many think it's in the back somewhere?" he asked, and still other participants raised their hands. "Okay," he said. "Now, look again" and he projected the slide for a few more seconds. "This time, did you notice that the hole was somewhere...different?" Lots of hands were raised, as people in the audience realized that they could not only see the hole on the first surface they saw it on, but on two or three other surfaces, as well. "Okay look one last time," Booker said, and turned the slide back on for good. He asked the participants to visualize the hole on every possible surface, front center, front lower right, back surface lower right, in the top surface looking down, and so on.

"Here's another thought," he said. "Maybe it's just a ball floating, and there's no hole at all!" Everyone laughed, and some people talked amongst themselves and pointed. Some people even argued with each other about what surface the hole was on and whether it was a hole or a floating ball. Booker regained their attention. "What does all this mean? What's the point here?" he asked as he strolled up and down the stage, taking a few responses from the audience. He continued, "All those interpretations you suggested are correct. This is an exercise that encourages seeing things from a different perspective with an open mind. However, the main lesson in looking at this box is what you just experienced. After seeing it in one or maybe two places initially, you were eventually able to see it in four, five, or even six possible places. Think about this, now—why were you able to? What enabled you to see other possibilities?"

Booker paused and listened to a few responses that were shouted out and then went on to answer his own question. "It's because you were *willing* to try to see a different perspective! How often is this lack of perspective or open-mindedness a problem for you, your boss, your team, and everyone else around you? You get it, right? This has everything to do with conflict, relationships, agreement, consensus, contemplation, and involving others, as well as other dynamics that we'll be hitting on here over the weekend."

"If you showed up skeptical, are you willing to see the hole in other places? Are you willing to see things beyond your current thinking? Are you open to the different perspectives you'll encounter here over the next two days? If so, we hope you will carry this open-mindedness with you as you go through the first breakout session, and the other sessions, too. I am confident that you will see great benefits if you do, and see some things from perspectives you hadn't considered before."

Booker fielded a few administrative questions at that point and then said, "We have plugged in a good break into the agenda, so please take your time getting to the first session. You can even take a moment to step outside and inhale some of that clean, crisp Missouri air if you'd like! Then please report to your first session on time. We have a lot to share with you and will need every minute of the time we have scheduled. Here's to a couple of Great Eight days, enjoying continual learning and improvement!" Booker toasted the crowed with a bottle of water from the podium, "To willingness, learning, challenges, and transformation!"

"Oh, and one last quick bit of information," he said, as the participants readied themselves to leave. "We have invited some friends to visit during the conference—professionals from related fields and sponsors. They will be available for you to network with and, of course, to make their services available to you. These are all people I trust and have good relationships with, so check them out. Some are from the local Kansas City area while others have traveled some distance to be here. Feel free to introduce yourself as you move between sessions. I'd like to introduce one to you now. Derek Kenner is a great friend of mine. He coauthored a book with me and he's got an amazing speaking and singing voice. I've asked him to sing a song of his as you depart. His contact information is up there on the screen and he just recently published his first book. Go for it Derek!"

Derek grabbed the microphone and said, "Thanks, Booker, for the invite. I would love to speak with any one of you. My book offers inspiring messages and affirmations that will comfort and guide you as you read them each day. Here's one of my favorites from the book that I will not really sing, in spite of Booker's encouragement. You will also hear a taped version, which is available at the booth, along with the book. Have a great conference one and all."

Mickey remained seated as Debra and Les stood, listened to the song for a few moments, and headed toward the back doors. She tried to reach Jackson but couldn't by either phone or text, so she called Doc. He answered and told Mickey that he had taken Chief back into the hospital for a follow-up examination. He wasn't sure, but it seemed as if the shock of the accident was causing some serious problems. Chief just wasn't improving as he should, but Doc still held out hope. Doc also told Mickey that one of Jackson's coaches had called and that Jackson was at a meeting with them now, but he'd make sure to have him call her when he returned.

Mickey was worried. After saying a quick prayer, she chased Les down and kissed him goodbye. She needed to catch her bus for the Lexington trip. As they parted, Les handed her a note about a bookstore in Lexington called the River Reader that he had found online. He asked her to pick up a book for him about Lexington's history. Les was a bit envious of Mickey—part of him clearly wished he was going with her.

Debra and Les decided that they would separate and work in different breakout groups. That way, they would each pick up different material and not influence each other during the sessions. They each hooked up with their respective groups, introduced themselves, and mingled in the lobby. Before they went to their breakout sessions, Les went over to Debra and arranged for them to meet outside the Sprint Center doors that faced the Power & Light District so they could have lunch together. They agreed to have lunch outside and enjoy the beautiful, sunny, warm spring weather.

Debra ducked into the restroom to throw out an empty coffee cup and then caught up with her group as they were browsing at a table of books in the lobby. A lady was purchasing a book from a local author. There was a poster advertising the book propped on an easel nearby.

Just then, Debra met a gentleman who like Watlington, was a friend of Booker's. He was greeting folks in the lobby; the conference was known for finding and inviting local leaders, educators, and businesspeople. In speaking with John, she discovered he was working on a book called *The Evolution of the African American Male and the Family Structure.* This interested Debra, so she grabbed a card of his.

During break, Les is caught up in a conversation with another of the conference sponsors, Tim Cash. Being an avid reader, Les gets info about Tim's business and asks Tim about a book he has been seeking.

"We sell new & used books for your reading pleasure."

Tim Cash, Owner

tmcash@msn.com
816.659.4508

www.half.com, terylcosystems

Breakout Session #1: Communicate

Communicate

- Visioning
- Chain of Command
- Upward Flow
- Teach and Educate
- YOUR Wisdom
- Absolutes and Values

The facilitator of Debra's first breakout session tried to get the group to relax as they sat down by telling a few jokes. Once they were settled, he told them, "Something all of the facilitators will caution you about is the fact that we are only hitting on the high points here. That is, there is a lot of depth to the Great Eight—many years and a lot of experience—which has been developed by a great number of people. Our hope is that you will understand the most important strategies by the end of the conference. There just isn't enough time to cover everything, however. We developed our curriculum by studying the practical application of our Great Eight concepts in-house at a variety of organizations. Each of the Eight could take up a full day or more of study, but we're only spending an hour or two. For this reason, forgive me if I seem to be a bit blunt. I need to keep us moving along in order to cover as much material as possible. I want you to get your money's worth out of this session."

As the participants nodded their heads, Liz from Uniondale, NY, coming from the furthest away, said, "I'm with you and in the spirit of time, I'd like to jump right into the first bullet about visioning. If it's okay, I'd like to share some experiences of mine. For me, visioning used to be just a useless drill that some consultant or other pushed on me—we've all been through that, I suppose. More often than not, it's not helpful, wastes time, and only involves the top executives. It doesn't mean much to anyone, except, maybe, the finance folks who had to find the money to pay for it or the maintenance worker who had to put their poster on the wall."

The facilitator paused and observed the other participants' reactions. A lot of hands went up, and he pointed to Deanna from Fayetteville, Arkansas, who was sitting three rows back. "Can I jump in, and say I understand you completely? I want to share what visioning is to me and how I do it." After the other participants nodded, Deanna continued, "After my initial attempts at supervision and management, and observing some of the same problems that Liz referred to, I began to do things differently. From day one in a new managerial role, I envision with my team about what the team will look like when we reach our potential. Everyone knows what the company does, what products we make, and what services we provide. No one cares about that. We have to make every member of the team care. For me that entails making sure that everyone on my team envisions what we want the team to become."

A round of discussion followed regarding how critical it was to teach leaders to facilitate visioning and to involve their team in the process. Visioning was discussed further, especially how to teach it. It's not just some drill for the president and senior managers to do. Like many other things, an organization should make sure that a bottom-up approach should be taken with the front-line leaders beginning the process and letting it work its way up to the top. A strong foundation will ensure that ultimately the pieces will fit together and hold.

The facilitator moved to the topic of communication. The woman seated next to Debra said, "This seems like a no-brainer, but let's ponder this a bit. Listening is something that most of us are weak at; it's a big issue with many leaders. At least, I know it is for me and it definitely is for my boss. I have come to realize that most managers are not great listeners. Since we are the experts in charge, why would we want to bother listening? We may choose to believe that none of us would think that way consciously, however, I believe that it is a phase that every leader goes through, and some of us get stuck in it. I am paraphrasing—I can't remember the quote verbatim—but I remember reading a Stephen Covey book in which he said something like, 'seek first to understand before trying to be first understood.' That concept really took hold of me, and I embrace it and find it useful as I manage. Sincerely done, it is a powerful communication tool for a leader. Also, to follow up on the last comments, listening should definitely be part of the envisioning process. We want to listen to each other about what we envision as we set goals."

Debra smiled and said, "Nicely said, new friend of mine. You made some great points." Many other people in the room echoed their agreement of what she had said about communication. An impeccably dressed man in the group said, "I have thought about the second and third bullets, about upward flow and chain of command. These issues seem to be a matter of the leader changing the way things work, including the corporate culture and the mindset of the employees. It is not about dictating but, as Debra and our other friend mentioned, it is about listening before you speak. You need to create a mindset that your people and their thoughts come first, then the leaders and their ideas—upward communication. What a *vision* that would be if we could create it!"

The group continued their discussion, but the facilitator cut them short. After a few moments of silence, he continued, "You are all correct. Communication involves creating respect for other people's ideas, opinions, thoughts, suggestions, and solutions. When I hear you first, and

I am the leader, I am developing a culture of upward communication as opposed to the top-down communication that we're all too familiar with. At the foundation of all of this we have a leader creating what we call a nonthreatening environment within the team. When leaders do this, they have an organization with a culture of open communication flowing in all directions. He clicked the remote, and a slide displayed on the screen.

> How do you get people to speak up and talk in groups, participate in meetings, and communicate freely and upwardly?
>
> Threatening environments often exist.
> Relationships must be right.
> Understand the impact we have on each other.
> Seek first to understand.
> Teams don't allow nonparticipation of members.

"So, let me share some thoughts here," the facilitator continued. "Our first bullet says, 'Threatening environments often exist.' Watch out for that the next time you ask a group for input. Observe the dynamics of the group when people speak up. People have different levels of self-esteem. The quiet ones are typically the ones that struggle with this issue since they may have had a negative reaction(s) to group participation in the past. Therefore they perceive such interactions as being more threatening than their peers do. Perhaps they encountered their first negative reaction back in elementary school, when they were excited, enthusiastic, and eager to be called on, only to be ridiculed for their idea."

"The second bullet, 'Relationships must be right,' alludes to getting serious about involvement, participation, and team problem-solving. Remember that all teams have problematic relationships within them—dominating people as well as insecure people who, perhaps, are newly hired. Negative practices that were used in the past must be addressed. Informal rules need to be put into place to create a new, safe starting point, one that encourages open communication."

"The third bullet is, 'Understanding the impact we have on others.' You, the leader, must make your team understand the damage that negative actions and words can do to others. Most of us have no intention of harming anyone, but it's possible to do so without even trying. Who decides if what you said or did hurt? The receiver, of course—their perception is their reality, regardless of what you meant. Once again, we see the importance of addressing relationships."

"'Seek first to understand,' is a concept we already covered thanks to our friend over here who shared her interpretation and application of Steven Covey's ideas, so we can move on to our final bullet, 'Teams don't allow nonparticipation of members.' Everyone on the entire team needs to be aware of who is and isn't participating. You, the leader, won't be able to observe all of your team's activity directly. Teach and place the responsibility on the team to police each other. This needs to be a part of the team's goal or vision; they need to accept responsibility for ensuring that each team member participates fully in order for the team to reach its potential."

Everyone in the session agreed that the information the facilitator had just shared with them was right on target and requested written materials to take home with them. "All of you will be getting a copy of a book which details everything you will learn in all of the breakout session upon your departure tomorrow. So, are there any other ideas about communication?"

Debra remembered something she had learned from Les a while back and spoke up. "A mentor of mine shared something with me that struck me as being an important communication issue in organizations. When we come out of meetings, we frequently mess up the chain of command flow of communication. That is, instead of taking notes in a meeting and quietly saving that information for the next meeting, I gather my team together and deliver that information to them right away. I don't let even a week go by without sharing newly acquired information. I get it to them right away before they hear it from someone else and wonder why I didn't tell them."

Everyone in the room nodded and recognized the important issue Debra had brought up. They discussed it further for a few minutes before the facilitator told them that they needed to move on to the next topic and projected a slide.

> Give a person a fish
> and they eat today.
> Teach a person to fish
> and they eat for a lifetime.

"Let me address something else that we need to cover. First, let me say that this has been a great discussion so far. You've all contributed ideas that have furthered everyone's learning. Thank you. Now, I really need to stress the importance of this point. Booker's first book, *Teaching Fishing*, is based on the idea up on the screen. The idea of teaching someone to fish has a lot to do with the leader-follower relationship, upward communication, and vision. It is a concept that we all preach and try to put into practice."

"Oh, by the way," the facilitator interrupted himself, "it's a bit off topic, but I just remembered something else I need to tell you. The conference just found out that the pastor who was supposed to speak tonight can't make it, so Booker will be speaking, instead. If you didn't sign up before, you ought to do so as soon as possible. You will enjoy what he has to say, trust me on this one," he smiled, knowingly. "You will be really glad that you did. You have until noon to register."

"Now, back to our slide—it's not talking about catching fish, but about catching people. It's a really useful concept to adopt. It's affected the way I lead and facilitate and I also teach it to and use it with my graduate-level students of business. It's about teaching people to think. Here's an example of how it applies to all of us leaders. You've probably heard a leader you know mutter something like, 'Day after day, I have people lined up at my door wanting to know about this or that. They want to know what to do about this or how to handle that; they want to know what I want them to do.' This sort of negative thinking drags the person on and on and they get caught up in it. Now look at the slide again and see if you can find a connection. You see, we fall into a trap as managers, leaders, or teachers when we attempt to handle, answer, and solve everything. You might say that we're handing out fish! Don't feel too bad if you recognize your own behavior—I'm here to help you overcome it. Our instinct is to do the right thing and help the people we're leading by giving them the answer. But some of you have probably surmised why giving out answers is a bad idea."

Kendra from Lenexa, Kansas interrupted. "If I may, teacher, I believe the next consideration is the issue that causes us, in real life, to fall into this trap—time! I've read Booker's first book, *Teaching Fishing*, so I'm familiar with this concept, although I still haven't mastered it.

It's very efficient to just give answers rather than getting our people to think and solve their problems themselves. You see, the quicker I give him or her an answer, the quicker I can give the next person a fish. Besides isn't that my job as the leader to do the thinking and make all the decisions, provide answers?"

The facilitator gestured at Kendra to continue on, stating that she was right on track. Kendra went on, "When we function this way, all we are doing is providing fish instead of teaching people to fish for themselves. Now we must ask ourselves this question, where will these same people come the next time they are hungry?"

After thanking Kendra, pausing to field a couple of questions and comments, the facilitator wrapped up, "This is what we use in training leaders and what we will be preaching, teaching and practicing right here in this conference. You will see this extensively practiced within each of your breakout sessions, watch for it. Think about it right here, where have the answers come from here? I am just asking the questions here for the most part. My team, you guys are delivering the answers...or many of them anyway! I go last, and wrap it up, adding anything I might need to, that's been left out or just to summarize and reinforce.

Develop the habit that when people come to you with problems, your response automatically is: WHAT WOULD YOU DO?   WHAT DO YOU THINK? HOW WOULD YOU DO IT? We believe here that this is one of those one things that could make a real difference in your leadership, if understood and practiced.

And then get ready to coach! What if it is a good solution? Now what if the idea is something that you know won't work?"

Hands went up with several responses and thoughts regarding these leading questions. "Oh and just one more thing before we jump topics here. There are tons of dynamics and plenty of understanding a leader should study and understand when using this practice. Do yourself a favor and go buy the book; it's only like ten bucks anyway.

So, what do you think?" The facilitator was grinning big as he gestured toward a hand in the back.

Bob from somewhere way up by the Nebraska, Kansas line, began sharing before someone else could, "Hey I got one for you, one of my pet peeves. An issue with management and organizations and all this."

With all focusing on Bob and wondering where he was going, he pressed on quickly, "Suggestion boxes, they have got to go. They are not suggestion boxes, but distrust boxes." Pausing to look around for a moment, Bob asked, "Consider what they say to people and what they represent?"

Debra had turned to look around and see Bob eye to eye, "I am with you here, wow as you said that, it just hit me hard. I know where you are going I think. But until just now, within the context of this *Communications* session, I never thought about them in that way before. In fact I was always a big proponent of them being put up! I believe as I think about them in the context of our discussions here, they are managers and management saying, we don't want you to talk to your leader; so go write your idea, suggestion, improvement comment, etc on a note and stick it in a box. Oh my gosh, that is so stupid!"

Just then, the facilitator assumed the lead, "Right you are. If leaders created a trusting and non-threatening world for their folks; then always encouraged upward communication; envisioned how we want to be; ...we wouldn't have any need for those stupid distrust boxes, would we?"

The lady by Debra smiled, "You got it my friend. I realized this also a while back; sold management and immediately got them taken down in our facility. Debra, I also used to think they were a great thing."

A lively discussion began to escalate as the facilitator jumped back into the mix before anything further could come up, "Sorry gang, but we have to begin wrapping up this session. I have to get you out of here in about eight or nine minutes. Let me just quickly hit on a few things we need to touch on and do a little summarizing. Let me share with you a couple of realizations that tie into some of what we just talked about along with the bullet up there about sharing wisdom."

He walked out amongst them sharing, "There is a natural inclination when someone moves into a leadership role, for him/her to assume they are there or they have arrived, when achieving that leadership role. This may or may not be a conscious awareness. Along with status, is a seemingly clear responsibility to *share your wisdom*? Our friend up here spoke of all this earlier when she was discussing the importance of listening. I just wanted to make sure we hit us all between the eyes with this reality.

This happens to not only managers in the workplace, but also occurs in politics, with teachers, in parenting, coaches, consultants, and again, any position of authority granted a person in some way. This thinking does not make he/she a bad person, it just is a matter of ignorance of the role, on their, our part. Caring leaders realize this and don't let themselves fall into this trap. Know any of these know-it-alls? Are you one, or were you at some point in time? Sounds extreme, know-it-all, but to the follower, student, employee, etc, that's how it can come across to them?

You see, when I am appointed to be the manager because I know *more than anyone else*, my seniority/experience/expertise, then I subconsciously believe this.

A very natural behavior follows – that of making decisions instinctively all on your own, not asking other's opinions, not involving the team, not keeping them informed, etc.   You are quickly becoming one of those *my way or the highway* kind of managers, purely unintentionally. Any newly appointed leader role *will* become one unless you have people to hold you accountable to *not be* one of *those*. Here's a tip in these regards: Those you lead are the best gage of this! Turn them loose on you!

In case it's not totally clear, if this isn't understood by you the leader, this happening is killing effective communications. Here's another twist just saying the same in a different way. If I know it all, you are the distributor of knowledge and wisdom, why would you listen, asks their opinion or how could you be encouraging upward flow?

Something as simple as the idea of *two heads being better than one* just sort of gets lost in the process; it becomes something that tends to fade from the manager's thinking. You have waited a long time to be in charge and so now, you get to make the decisions, right? You get it? Alright then, we absolutely have to end this."

Debra stood, saying, "I have to confess something and thank you. I am one of those skeptics Booker was speaking about. When I saw this Great Eight thing, I had some serious doubts. Those doubts are not all gone believe me, but let me share this about this first session.

When I saw the *Communicate* concept, I thought to myself this would be a bunch of communication definitions, steps and well simple stuff we all learned in our first days of ever supervising anyone. I figured on a bunch of basic supervisory skill stuff....Sender-Receiver stuff, have people repeat things back to you, communication barriers, 5 keys to effective communications, blah, blah, blah.

At least to this point, this has really been what it was sold to be: application, more on strategic understanding, human behavior, depth, clarify, solving problems that are real, etc. I'm still processing, but just wanted to say thanks to you our facilitator and all of you here for some thought-provoking ideas, and learning." Debra looked at the facilitator as she sat back down, receiving a thumbs up gesture, a positive nod and a big smile. "And seven more to go, how's that for the right attitude!"

Before completely wrapping up, Robin from Iron Mountain, MI shared something interesting about organizational structure, "Organizational structure seems to me to be one of the most significant issues impacting organizational communications." She paused for a moment, "Consider the organizational chart? What I came across a while back was that frequently we change it to meet the demands of personalities and people problems, instead of organizing to accomplish the mission. It was probably another one of those struggles I brought into management from my military experience. Mission first, then organize people to support the mission; for us that's all about making the product, providing your service, etc. When we move people around, along with their functions because of bad relations and conflicts, the result is that we are creating functional conflicts, along with confusing logical communication channels, pathways and the information flow. Did I make any sense with that?"

The facilitator jumped in, "Let me finish this up with a couple of points, so I can get you guys out of here, seriously. Great stuff by the way, appreciate you bringing that up, nice job. Indeed our people system should be designed to support the business vs. re-designing the operation to support the people issues! So many companies have been changed so much to meet the personality quirks... that the lines of communication, information flow, etc in fact don't make sense anymore. Systems and processes have become very confused. People get frustrated because nobody understands it... because it, the structure doesn't make sense."

The facilitator was shaking his head and chuckling as he walked to the other side of the room, "We all here, now and then discuss how real this is and how several years back someone sold the management world on this being okay. They put a consulting and marketing spin on it and labeled it a Matrix organizational structure. You guys have heard of that but likely never really knew what it was about, did you? You shouldn't, it makes no sense, well unless you are looking for an excuse why your structure is messed up! Now you have a label and name for it! They tossed away the old organizational structure with some platitudes, made-up logics and reasoning to sell their consulting value I imagine. They sold this bill of goods as one that made sense as long as you called it by another name. Throw out the org chart and just call it Matrix. What is so funny to me, is having watched the movie Matrix, once years ago, it didn't make sense; they labeled this thing correctly, because it also is nuts and makes no sense.

Before anyone jumps in here, I realize many people to include you may have loved the movie; regardless it was still about some complicated, dynamic and confusing stuff". The facilitator acknowledged some comments still chuckling and smirking at the idea.

"Lastly, and we really don't have any time to go into it, but in sorting out communication issues, you and your organization need to look at just how does the chain of command and management team distribute information? Do we rely on bulletin boards, memos, town hall meetings to the masses, emails, faxes? Have we forgotten the significance of verbal, one-on-one communication? How effective are our meetings? Is communication effective in all directions or do we just send directions downward?"

The *Communication* principle had really been covered well. Everyone agreed on that, as the facilitator concluded and wrapped up.

Finally, walking over and opening the door, he continued, "Lastly, I believe you will start seeing that all of these dynamics surrounding the Great Eight are very much overlapping. You will see how all eight will inter-connect before this time tomorrow. That is about real learning, repetition, real understanding and internalizing; which as we all know is critical to real behavioral change and real learning. You will likely think now and then how something you are talking about in one breakout could actually fit in a different breakout. Let me assure you, you are probably right. We are aware of this. Again, this is one of the keys to this learning working and sticking. Thanks for your focus, time and effort here one and all, good meeting you; good learning with you.

Oh, oh, oh, there is one more 'one last thing'" smiling big as he moved back to the front, grabbing a sheet of paper, waving it. "Grab this sheet out of your packet."

Communicate: Great 8 Connections & 'food for thought'...

Notice how the other seven concepts support, reinforce, and connect with this one.

RELATE   If the relationship isn't good, the communication won't be, either.

EVALUATE   Evaluate the challenges and barriers to good communication.

CREATE   Improved relationships and new systems enhance communication.

ELIMINATE   Get rid of the obstacles of good communication— physical, emotional, and relational.

FACILITATE   Make it easy for people to interact with each other when making decisions and solving problems.

ACCOMMODATE   Be receptive and available to people and their ideas and suggestions.

DEMONSTRATE   Model open, trusting, and risk-free communication with everyone in all directions.

Please make your own notes and comments below.

"Here's the deal with this Connections sheet, and this will make more and more sense as you move through your sessions. As part of the learning process, we want you to realize how each of the eight reinforce and well, work with the others. This can tend to go right over your head if we don't focus on it a bit. Let me share with you just a little before I kick you out of here, how this works. Again, you will get a similar summary at the end of each breakout, to help you see how it is all intertwined; how all the principles work to support the others. Internalized and then practiced, this becomes some pretty powerful leadership stuff my friends. Okay so fairly quickly let me just reinforce a few things here which are already spelled out somewhat for you, there on the sheet."

The facilitator took a few minutes and a few questions in clarifying and connecting the dots (all 8 principles). There were some definite 'ah has' from a few; there were also some puzzled looks from some others. It would totally make sense to all by the end of the conference; learning of all eight and then having them connected as just happened here.

He took a couple of admin questions as all gathered their materials, stood and headed out; most stopped and shook hands with the facilitator first. They were left with a quote flashed up on wall:

> More often than not -
> people, leaders and
> organizations are not
> really challenged by
> **COMMUNICATION**
> issues, ...but by
> **RELATIONSHIP** issues.

Warren Wandling was a local businessman and entrepreneur helping host the event and was shaking hands and greeting people as they departed their first breakout session.   As his business was a logical tie-in, he handed out several requested biz cards to folks.

Debra had numerous Ah-ha moments during the first session and realized her communication style may be impacting her team's performance, as well as both her professional and personal life.

She realized that her team would produce better results, more efficiently and with less rework if she modified her communication style and practices. The infighting within the team as well as absenteeism, and overall morale were certainly areas she could see improving as well.

She was excited and did some quick back of the envelope math. With a conservative approach she scratched out:

Debra's Notes about ROI after Breakout #1

If I could gain a 2-5% increase in efficiency and reduce rework by 2-5%, I would improve department performance by 5%!

If any changes reduced the chronically high use of unplanned time off (which is now 5-10% daily), the department performance would easily improve by/to... 10%.

If I have to change something in me, does that mean that I've been a bad leader? With these modifications of behavior, will the company think less of me? Will I make myself expendable and be seen as a loser that needed to change their leadership style?

Or do I need to keep changing in order to continue growing? Doesn't a real leader continually grow/improve?

Have my poor or failed relationships caused me to behave inappropriately? Have I said things that have driven people away—even people I was close to? People I needed? It is, indeed, true that by modifying my style I could produce better, more positive business results. Would I also enhance my professional image in improving my personal relationships?

All of this seems to be a (3) benefit improvement for a (1) modification improvement—a 3:1 ROI. That's worth it, for sure!

Am I up to the task of going through with it?............

Breakout Session #2: Relate

Relate

- 360 Degrees
- Socializing
- The HEART First
- Boss and Buddy
- 24 x 7
- Trust Barriers

"Greetings," said Ms. Douglas, the facilitator as she clicked the remote and displayed a slide on the projection screen. As people were settling in, she said, "This second breakout goes over the critical factors necessary when it comes to utilizing the power of relationships.

This for sure touches every other breakout session's content. I want to challenge you to think as we move along here; how everything we speak to here will likely tie back for sure to your last session, *Communications*."

Ms. Douglas was a loving proud lady who everyone immediately took to; she didn't really ask or insist to be called by her full name, it just happened that way. She shared a bit about being from the D.C. area, a distinguished tenure in the military and tons of training time in various venues. She was affiliated with a Human Resources professional organization of some sort - neat person.

"I know you heard this in the beginning of your first session, but I will also briefly remind you that there is much to this topic, too much for our brief time together. We have done in-house leadership work at times for a couple of days, just on this one great eight principle.   We will try to hit the key points here and leave you with some good strategic understanding; some angles maybe you never thought much about; and demonstrate how it applies to your role as leaders."

As people were locking in on the facilitator, Debra was really chewing on this one about befriending those you lead – the bullet up there on Boss & Buddy. She and Les had argued this on many occasions. To her, this was always thought to be something you just didn't do. However as promised, as she sat there, she was trying to be open minded. This concept was hitting home with her, as she considered her relationships at work and well, in life in general. Her divorce, as divorces tend to do had blown up her small circle of friends leaving maybe just one or two good friends in her life. Other than Les and Mickey she really didn't have many people around her she would consider close friends.   That's pretty sad she thought, as she peered around the room looking at the faces of others. She thought how important relations really are, when you think of how much of our lives we spend with those we work. She also was picturing her team, her people, individual personalities and their situations. Honestly Debra didn't really know much about most on her team. She did have a fairly high level of turnover, making relationships challenging. She thought how, other than the superficial stuff, she just didn't know her folks. For sure she wasn't close to any one of them. That's sad, she thought; no that's probably stupid; and I'm in charge!

Sarah, Franklin and Ana, three of her longest tenured employees had also suffered through marriage breakups since the time Debra had taken over as manager. Was she there for them and would it have been nice if they could have been there for me?

Before Ms. Douglas uttered another word, Debra decided to broach this topic, "If I may, I would like to reflect a bit on a personal level in addressing the bullet up there about Boss & Buddy. I'm just sitting here thinking of my own sad life, probably could be called dysfunctional to include a divorce within the last year. I am picturing my people and how I really don't know them well. For sure there is some dysfunction with some of my people that I know of, but not much. Sad, when you think of work being where they, I mean we, spend most of our lives. It is there, I mean our, real source for relationships, isn't it?

I'm also sitting here processing this point, this idea and what it would mean if the relationships between me and my people were good ones? Furthermore, what it would mean if I could somehow help them to really like and develop close friendships with those they work with day in and day out?"

Ms. Douglas cut in, "Debra, we all believe here that what you are considering is something that would make amazing differences in you, your team and your productivity. For you and others, likely even in your personal worlds. Let me also assure you, you are not the Lone Ranger with this; we have discovered many, and maybe most managers just won't go there. They won't focus on and build those relationships. Bad stuff happened to them by past ineffective leadership and managers, and so...

We'll be all over this topic Debra, so hang in there and make sure we deal with your point and issues here. Now before taking any more questions let me share with you some aspects of this TRUST thing, the breakdowns that impact our relationships, and well, trust! Debra we will get back to this in different ways, I promise. Hold me to that will you, trust me?" The facilitator smiled big, clicking her remote, displaying:

- "Quality first" lies
- Workload and scheduling promises
- Shooting the messenger
- We want risk takers!
- Unfair promotions, raises, and transfers
- "Let me check on it and get back to you"
- Failing to deliver on commitments
- Ignored and ridiculed ideas and opinions
- Gossiping about coworkers after meetings
- Not confronting problems as they occur
- Hidden agendas: control, manipulation
- Not getting timely information
- Cliques and subgroups circumvent the team!

"We hear trust discussed by leaders frequently, don't we? We fear it's not deeply understood by leaders and for sure poorly demonstrated in practice. Let me share about a few of these bullets here. We all agree that trust is important, and although we don't intentionally lie, your leadership team (or chain of command) may be creating a culture of Distrust. Here are a few ways that we fail to tell the truth. I am going to just run through these and then we can discuss, hang with me just a few minutes.

The old Quality First preaching, this is a *biggee*... we preach this, print it on Values cards, place it within our Vision/Mission statements, put it on walls and then tell people to shut up and ship it after identifying a problem, flaw, etc. Think how your organization or how you even might do this?

And how about Workload and Scheduling promising. We say things like, 'We won't be working Saturday, or we won't be working late tonight' These are common ploys of leaders to keep people motivated until later in the day/week when we drop the surprise bomb on them and work after all!

That's real motivating alright?" as the facilitator looked out for acknowledgements. She was seeing plenty of smirks, positive nodding and even a few Amen's."

After fielding a few comments, she went on, "Time after time, we make decisions and provide solutions or fish for them to execute; having never consulted with them, asked their opinions or attempted to gain buy-in. Yet we are all along preaching about teamwork, yikes.

Tell us when you see a problem or issue, the ol' shooting the messenger thing. We ask for the truth, but when it turns out to be bad news or criticism we don't like to hear, we blow them away. Maybe we are indeed 'shooting the messenger' By the way; this is a great way to prevent information from getting to you. Indeed it is frequently why we put up suggestion boxes?"

Everyone looked, smiling and pointing at Bob, and the lady next to Debra. After hearing the group had hit on the suggestion box issue in the last session, Ms. Douglas continued, "So we're on the same page with getting rid of those boxes huh? So how about Risk-Takers! Frequently we abuse, ignore, ridicule, or in other ways, put down people for having taking risks.

Are you starting to see how big of a deal this trust thing actually is in your organization or on your own teams? Think any of this might just be impacting working relationships in all directions?

How about promotions, raises, and transfers? How many times do you think that someone in your organization has considered himself or herself to be the right person for the job, only to have given it to someone else? When we don't have a system for evaluating performance, people will consider your system unfair... and it probably is! We'll hit this hard in the *Evaluate* session, so we'll just leave it here for now.

Here's the deal, you are building an environment of it's not what you know, but who you know! And why do we have to make such a secret about pay? Organizations even at times discipline people for talking about pay, salary, etc. What's up with that, as if we don't know? It's all about you, us, management in general, not doing it fairly; so we have to keep it hush-hush, right? And we all know that everyone really does talk about it, feel it is unfair, know it is unfair, and trust gets worse and worse...

Ever said to someone, 'Let me check on it, and I'll get back to you?' I heard this dynamic connected to something called the Monkey concept several years ago. Take a moment and think how many times you have heard this said to people, or had someone say it to you? Now think about what happened when you or they failed to get back to the person? I'm not suggesting that you, or that manager intentionally lied, but isn't it the same thing to that person? You are going to forget, so outsmart yourself. Here's a huge leadership survival tip: give them the right to pester you until you get back to them. Trust me, if you take that monkey on your back and forget they will believe you lied and that you do not care! Failing to deliver on commitments or deadlines, all the same thing huh?

Wrapping this trust thing up, I have just a couple more points to mention. How about ideas and opinions not acted upon? How about people's thoughts being discounted, not explored, ignored or being laughed at?

One of my pet peeves and absolutes with teams I have led is the issue of gossiping and/or talking about each other outside of meetings! I believe it was Covey also that I am referencing here, he called it 'disloyalty to the absent'. Tied closely to this is the more subtle behavior of just sharing stuff about someone to others? Taking a message to the wrong person? It's relevant to every one of us—we've all seen it...done it...and had it 'done' to us as well! This goes on all the time, but if you and your team can get hold of this one...enormous strides can be made toward increased teamwork, trust, less conflict, more productivity and improved relationships all the way around."

Debra cut in, "Consider this scenario and thinking, my boss shared this with me. You have a problem with someone (what they said, what you thought they said, and their opinion, something they did that impacted your world, etc...get the picture?) What do we typically do when this occurs? We go share it with someone else—a peer, a boss, everyone except the person who really needs to hear it! Starting to connect, aren't you?

Teammates (employees within the same office-under the same leader) frequently will even take it straight to the leader to deal with. Think of the impact and fallout of doing things this way--first of all, the person you are taking it to can do nothing but listen to your bellyaching. What are you expecting them to do with it? If they go do something with it, then they have broken your trust!?! If you allow them (or push them to do it for you) all you are going to do is lose respect and your relationship with that individual."

Ms. Douglas interrupted with, "Two last comments here and we'll get to answer your questions or points hanging out there. I see some hands up and I will get to you in just a minute.

Pass information to your people and do not ever try to keep something a secret. When people find out through the rumor mill or from the floor, what does it say about you their leader? Let me share you another issue that occurs along these lines. If the CEO or president or really any leader with his/her leaders says at anytime, 'keep this to yourself, keep it quiet for now' or words to this effect, you have just caused some further distrust. Think about it and also realize this – this quiet stuff is going to get out. Someone is going to tell someone and there it goes all over the place, isn't it?   Here's another final twist to doing this keeping things quiet attempt. When 'the secret' goes all over down and then back up to your manager, the one you told to be quiet, and then their employee asks them about it, what position have you put them in?"

The friend next to Debra blurted out along with some others, "Now they have to lie to that employee or tell them, breaking trust with you, the boss who told them to be quiet about it?"

The facilitator acknowledged and someone in the back made a reinforcing point, as Ms. Douglas concluded the trust thing, "Well I imagine we have beat this horse to death and you all have recognized most of these. Likely these are trust breakdowns you may have caused, seen others cause or that your company or organization has going on maybe daily, don't you?"

Following plenty of affirmations and acknowledgements, Alicia with MEPS in KC, spoke up for the first time, "If we are indeed finished beating that horse, can I offer another point on this relationship issue?"

The facilitator nodded smiling, as Alicia said, "I want to reconnect with the discussion we had earlier. I believe if you are a real leader, you will want to be around your people not just at work but in other aspects of their, your life. I am a believer in and say socialize with them, there is hardly any way to improve relationships quicker! This includes the willingness to be with people at anytime of the day - not just at work, but at play, after work, with families, socializing, etc. Of course, we as leaders all know that we have to invite all along of course. If you do socialize with one more than others, we just have to be big time conscious and make very sure there are no indicators or reasons for anything to look like favoritism while at work. In fact, for me personally, I have two people who everyone knows I am close to outside of work. When I took over as manager, I told them that I would not allow anything to appear wrong. In fact, they probably get dumped on by me, more work even unfairly placed on them just to prevent any appearance of favoritism.

Just curious how others view this issue?" asked Alicia, sipping her Diet Coke. There was plenty of discussion on this, and the facilitator made a few great points to help all see the value of socializing. The overall consensus seemed to be to do it, but always use caution.

Greg, a director over a public roads utility in North Kansas City somewhere, threw this in as that discussion calmed down, "Just my opinion and I believe something that has bunches to do with relationships; don't be one of those leaders who tell their people to leave personal business and problems at the front door. Let me just be blunt here, that is a load of crap, pardon my French.   Humans don't and can't do that; disconnect totally from their personal issues of life. Actually that includes you the leader, me, and every leader. Remember, you also have a boss and leader and do you really want a boss that says I don't care about you and your personal problems? Oh and also, Jesus the ultimate leader wouldn't not care. He would be there for people and their problems huh?"

Ms. Douglas acknowledged Greg's point, saying "Lordy mercy, I am so absolutely 100% with you guys. This point goes way beyond this and includes just knowing your people; it ties in obviously with the point Alicia just talked about. Spend time and every moment that you can to uncover, discover and express your concern for their world. Then you are a leader, to me anyway. After all, don't we all want that place where we spend so much of our lives to be a comfortable, family-oriented and friendly place where I matter,…where my problems matter?"

"That was awesome and well said my friends", coming from Kathy, a senior management rep from a major retailer in Tempe, AZ. "Before we get off this, let me add this, something that I have been thinking about since walking in here.   Relationship building involves recognition and praise of your people. Give praise in public settings; whether they want it or not; some will say they don't want that or don't like it. Do it anyway, that's just me, I'm doing it. And as we all have heard and need to keep in mind - you praise people in front of others and criticize in private. We all know that one but we need to keep it fresh; it is easy to mess up with that especially if you are in a high-pressure company like I know I am.

If you will give me just a couple more seconds, let me share something that happened to me maybe 20 years ago when I was a Second Lieutenant in the Army. This has stuck with me all this time. For those of you who may not know, a Second Lieutenant (2LT) is more or less, a frontline supervisor in our civilian organizations. Anyway I was this young 2LT, and although I assure you I didn't do too many things right, I did something special this one time, and my Commander, or my boss praised me. Now he didn't just praise me on his own or in front of a few of my peers, but in a conversation with his boss present. Ponder this for a moment. I cannot really explain why this was such a big deal, but trust me it was and is. It is one thing to receive recognition from your boss, but when he or she does so in front of his or her boss, it takes it up a notch. Trust me on this one! I just wanted to share that with the group", she said smiling and looking at faces around.

"This isn't exactly where we are and maybe a negative twist on all this. Still, I wanted to toss this in as it is one of my pet peeves and issues with some managers," Annette, a strong person of faith and neat lady from Fayetteville, NC jumped in before anyone else, and there were plenty with hands up. "First off, just wanted to second your thought Greg about Jesus. Also, we leaders should be recognizing exceptional performance, not the expected stuff. I take the time to recognize the deserving people, actions, results and accomplishments. This is not some watered-down lacking meaning program where everyone gets recognized, but truly is about recognizing those who have gone *above and beyond*. This is clearly laid out 'what is above and beyond' in his/her performance appraisal process. And because you care, you are doing each month, month in and month out. It's not the stuff that is part of the Performance

Appraisal process – that is the expected stuff. What we are talking about here is an employee doing the unexpected!

The facilitator cut in, "Very well said Annette and a super duper transition to your next breakout session on *Evaluation*; so we can just let it end there, because we must. Wow, this has been a great session. It's a bummer but we are going to have to wrap up." People began gathering their stuff, a few standing up already.

"As we move toward ending this session, let me leave you with this conversation with a supervisor in a Leadership Training session many years ago. I was an independent consultant and trainer; in about our fifth hour of training discussions. In the middle of a discussion much like this one probably, this guy named Rodney blurts out 'I think I just figured out why I don't like supervising. I really just don't like people'.

Everyone laughed a bit as the facilitator concluded with a smile, "It is kind of funny but also kind of sad? I am like you in thinking that Rodney was truly onto something here; what do you think? Effective leaders like people; there is no way around this. We agree?" He paused looking for nonverbal communication such as facial expressions, acknowledgements, and so forth.

"The sad part here is that it is amazing to think, isn't it, that we could have such a lack of understanding of what we (the organization) want in managers; that we could not even somehow check this out first?!? Anyone here resemble that thinking of Rodney's?" All looked around, but no one confessed if indeed this were the case.

"EVERYTHING in this conference – every tip, every lesson, every point, every conversation centers on the importance of the relationship first and foremost.

So often, managers tend to only begin working on the relationship-piece, after things have gone badly. Relationship needs to come first.

Let me offer you a tip I always suggest to leaders. When you are in your beginning days in a leadership role, and you are trying to figure it all out; what a great time to be working on relationships. Sure there will be meetings to go to, knowledge to gain, systems and processes to sort out, but just think about it. While you are ignorant anyway, why not learn, grow and build relationships with the people?   And the people here include every individual on your team, and also your boss, and every other internal customer that you or your team works with…!

Have a cup of coffee with someone before you need them or they need you!   Ponder that and what a great idea? Stuff will happen, and when it does, it is always a better result when you had a solid relationship with the individual beforehand.

Maybe you are well into your days and role in a leadership position. Maybe you didn't take this advice and you are paying for it now?   It's not too late, it all still holds true. It is just a different twist on the point; go fix, or rebuild those relationship(s) before any further time passes.

Okay, so this is really the last thing, because I must kick you out of here. I want to share with you guys, something I use in working with teams as a way of challenging them in this area.   Maybe this will be a good tip to leave you with…we refer to it here as *fixing the worst relationship*.

Take a team of ten people, maybe your team of ten that you lead. Each person is to look around the room at the team and decide who the worst relationship they have on that team is.   Now this doesn't have to be someone they have an issue with, although most of the time that is the dynamic in all likelihood.   It could just be someone they just know the least about or a new person on the team. Regardless all decide and you ask them/give them one month to go FIX IT! You challenge them and even them accountable to this, with your leadership and facilitation capabilities fully functioning. With persistence this can really accomplish a ton. Consider that first month and all those relationships improved what would that mean? What would it mean to the bottom line, not to mention just the environment? And then, the following month, and the following month we continue to work on these worst relationships?

So there you go, and before we completely leave that thought, how about you doing this *worst relationship* thing on your own level--with your peers, team-mates, co-managers, etc?

Alright, alright, no more *last things,*...well maybe just one! As you saw in your first session and will see in each of the eight, here is your Connections summarization. If you will take one of these sheets I am passing around, we'll look at it quickly."

Relate: Great 8 Connections & 'food for thought'…

Notice how the other seven concepts support, reinforce, and connect with this one.

EVALUATE …relationships, networks, inter-department interactions, and the chain of command—always.

CREATE …new relationships for you and those you lead— connections, opportunities.

ELIMINATE …conflict, bottlenecks, and breakdowns—identify and resolve them immediately.

FACILITATE …new relationships and introductions within and among your networks.

ACCOMMODATE …time for new, current, and past relationships. Always seek new relationships.

DEMONSTRATE …powerful, productive and positive relations in every direction.

COMMUNICATE …relationships are not maintained without interaction and communication.

Please make your own notes and comments below.

Some good discussion occurred with more eyes opening up, understanding how the principles were indeed tied together.

"Awesome folks, this was awesome—you were awesome! I hope you took away much to consider and go act upon. Thanks, and never hesitate to holler if I can help in your world; you have my contact information as well as that of all the facilitators in your packet.

Take care, God bless and enjoy the rest of the conference. You guys are heading over there to ROOM 10b, which will kick off in about 11 minutes it looks like."

The quote on the screen as people departed and others wandered in:

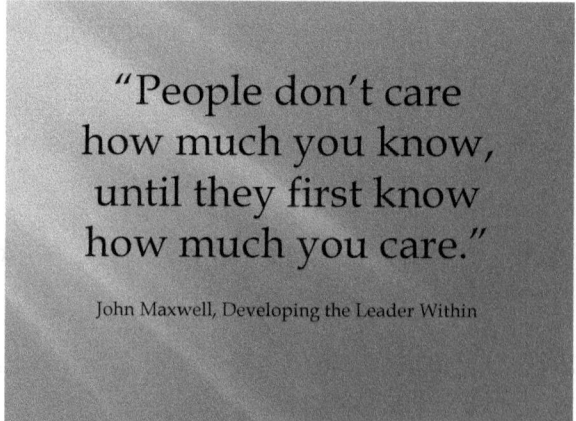

"People don't care how much you know, until they first know how much you care."

John Maxwell, Developing the Leader Within

Debra was recapping the dialogues in her mind and flip flopped between her inner voice of doubt telling her that what she was learning was all *pie in the sky* and *consultant speak* without any real world foundations. Then the rational side of her mind blocked out those skeptical thoughts to focus on adopting some of these changes. What the facilitator and group were proposing, would it really work?   And was there either a business or personal benefit or reward for her to make the change?   She went down the list...

Debra's Notes about ROI after Breakout #2

This boss and buddy thing—my group doesn't share much of their lives with me and I'm not sure they want to. Besides, it's unprofessional—isn't it? I am thinking that I do, indeed, have a boss and buddy relationship with my own boss! Without that trusted relationships and mentorship I would not have survived in that company, especially when I was going through my divorce.

Networking, socializing, and trust—while I have some professional relationships, I also know that I could improve my relationships with peers and other employees in the company. My attitude is especially bad with the HR Manager. There are numerous instances where my lack of a good relationship with a coworker has caused problems and possibly a lack of support. It's likely the reason why I have experienced resistance when trying to champion something or make something happen—stupid! I just socialized with the boss (at Mulligan's) just before we came here and that sort of thing really strengthens our relationship.

Some other people in the company, especially managers, seem to have an easier time getting things done. I wonder if I invested in meaningful relationships (which would require eating some crow) and developed rapport and trust with people if I would be a more effective leader. How would this behavior modification produce tangible results?

ROI? The amount of time I spend inspecting every result throughout the day and having to make corrections to production. I am always on my team to produce the right results because I feel as if I can't trust them without watching them throughout the day. I easily spend 25% of my day doing this inspection. Les would call it micromanaging! What would I do with my time if 25% of my workday freed up>

If I develop professional relationships on the basis of trust, connection, and genuine respect for people I could easily free up 80% of my inspecting time to work on relationships, employee engagement in problem solving, and process improvements to have people who are doing the work be accountable for their performance. I could utilize scorecards that reflect employee performance. With an established relationship, I would be able to effectively coach and develop my team to focus on the department's productivity. Other beneficial examples come to mind as I think of how interdepartmental improvement could be made with positive financial results. Relations with other departments that I fight with all the time—what would improvement there mean to us, me, and the company overall?

+++++

Darek Dubsky, a long time friend of the conference and golf pro stopped by the conference at lunch to say hello. Darek and Booker have partnered up in the past to do personal leadership and team development on the golf course. It is a concept and now a business Darek markets on top of his other work, called LEADERSHIP LINKS of KC. Booker introduced Darek during lunch and nearly immediately he had a small group of people walk up to Darek talking golf.

The weather was right and Darek actually left with some spouses of conference attendees, heading to the links. He signed up seven conference attendees interested in going out this evening for a quick nine holes. He handed out several business cards to folks interested in maybe utilizing the services with their companies.

Breakout Session #3: Evaluate

People were pretty wired and still discussing the last session when the facilitator broke in, "Before we begin, I am handing you a copy of something that was supposed to get to you in the last session. She said you guys got so deep into things; she just never got to this. It more or less speaks for itself; it's just a thing but a good thing with some pretty thought provoking thoughts." He finished distributing them ending back up front.

Everything Leaders Need to Know

If we live with **criticism**: We learn to **condemn**.
If we live with **hostility**: We learn to **fight**.
If we live with **ridicule**: We learn to be **shy**.
If we live with **shame**: We learn to feel **guilty**.
If we live with **tolerance**: We learn to be **patient**.
If we live with **praise**: We learn to **appreciate**.
If we live with **fairness**: We learn **justice**.
If we live with **approval**: We learn to like **ourselves**.

If we live with **acceptance** and **friendship**:
We find the world and workplace to be **good** and **positive**!

• What is our organization living, teaching, and practicing? What are our leaders doing?

•Many leaders and managers in our organizations did not necessarily live and learn from a good role model regarding the treatment and leading of people. Therefore, organizations have a very high likelihood of the wrong "stuff" being modeled unless we very clearly address the right principles and values through our people-development processes.

"From your comments I overheard as you came in, we must be causing some real thinking to go on here. Am I right in my assumption?" heads nodded affirmatively as he clicked the remote displaying the *Evaluate* session content.

Evaluate

- Self FIRST
- Mentor and Coach
- TEAM Competencies
- Fix versus Fire
- Annual Drill Gone
- ETA 'Everywhere, everyone'

"Now jumping right into our topic here, whether you realize it or not, most leaders, maybe including some of you right here, do not evaluate effectively and even avoid it.   We believe this failure or lack of real assessment is normally more about the leader's issues, procrastination, insecurities, lack of tools, hesitancy to honestly input and desire to avoid confrontation and conversation.   Think about this; as we discuss things here, how can anyone improve without input?   How does anyone learn without some teaching, facilitation, coaching, direction, guidance, etc?

If that's not enough, how about this …it's your job!   Also realize this, your people won't care so much that it is not happening until too late; when they get some feedback that is not so good.   It is when you have to do it …like at the end of the year or when something gets so bad that it has to be dealt with, now they care.   Been there done that; maybe from both directions? No one cares too much until you surprise them with an unfair assessment! Think about it now, whether it is right on or not, it is unfair. Think on that for a moment!

What we are suggesting is whether you are new to leadership or if you have been at it for a while and aren't doing it ...starts now. No matter what, in the beginning of the process between two people, discussing performance, and improvement and behavior flaws ...it will be a bit tough. Again, this mindset of feedback being a *bad thing* is for you to get changed, through your leadership.   Once it is done routinely, these conversations become much easier.   Consider the issues, suggestions and the model provided here in giving you some tools to do this well, effectively and in a caring way."

The facilitator paused here to take comments and questions. There were plenty. Pressing on after responding to a few, "We believe--and I am sure you will agree--that leaders should provide clear expectations and standards from the very beginning."Whether we are speaking of your employee's overall job performance or a task/action you are delegating, expectations and accountabilities need to be clear.

I want to share with you something one of our consultants ran across listening to a leader in a company many years back. We have adopted it, altered it slightly and preach and teach it.

It is a concept we refer to as ETA. ETA is about expectations, trust and accountability; here's how it works. We spend the time upfront clarifying in great detail expectations, standards and goals.   We discuss trust as it will play out during the process; I will trust you to holler if you are off track, need help or anything else begins to go wrong. You can trust that I won't watch over your shoulder, not trusting you are doing what we agreed. Lastly according to our agreed upon expectations, which *we* may have altered along the way as necessary, I will hold you accountable for the results.

Now, in the same light, if this is about the annual performance process, this means that we will spend considerable amount of time in January, assuming a calendar year situation …clarifying, discussing, and negotiating expectations, in specific measurable ways. We want total clarity regarding what we want the employee to make happen this year regarding performance. In February, we pull out the agreement and talk to the expectations as if it were the end of the year. In other words, 'if it were next December, here is how I would rate you …however it's not, so this just means we need to be working to improve in these areas, …and the good news is you have ten more months to correct!'

Make sense? We will do this talk in plenty of detail, again as if it were the end of the year, each month. The first few months will likely be a bit lengthy and uncomfortable. This will change as you lead the process demonstrating that this is not some negative drill but a fair and productive way to do business. By the end of the year, guess what? Right you are, you can and will provide a fair, accountable, easy and caring assessment of the employee. Because you cared, you spent the time to do this fairly and effectively."

Janelle from Heber Springs, Arkansas, just north of Little Rock, jumped in quickly, "You are so right, so many leaders to include my own boss do all this so poorly. Glad he's not here," she said with a sheepish grin looking around. Continuing she stood facing most all, "I want to share some beliefs I have regarding how evaluation, feedback and input are tied to an issue near and dear to all of us, turnover.

By focusing on real effective evaluation, you will seriously help your turnover; what I believe anyway. Something that I learned from a Business Coach I had a while back was put to me this way. Whether we are speaking of the Small Business Owner or the large corporation, hiring and firing people or turnover hurts in a ton of ways. There is nothing new about that, although rarely is the root cause really understood. Although many leap first to the hiring the wrong person rationalization, this is frequently not the actual cause. With all the efforts put into hiring, this just isn't the major issue here. Organizations and our HR folks are doing a lot of wringing of hands over making the decision who to hire, which is for sure smart! This process can take weeks and even months, and may include assessments, personality profiling, testing, stressing, and multiple interviewing...so better hiring just isn't the solution to turnover. A piece of it, yes no doubt.

The problem is the failure of leadership dealing with these fresh, enthusiastic, ready to go employees! Leadership is failing to provide routine, frequent feedback ....especially in the beginning to the newbie. Instead, when things go south, management just writes it off as another bad hire. Here's a story shared with me to demonstrate.

The coach I mentioned shared a story about someone he called Blake, a small business owner. Blake and his partner were doing well and had the business growing, and decided to hire someone to help out in this small service-oriented business. Blake had taken nearly six weeks speaking and interviewing several potential new hires. Lots of deliberation occurs before finally taking the plunge and hiring Ebony. Blake and his the partner was ecstatic about what all Ebony is doing in the initial days/weeks. Seemingly with very little guidance, she is just being everything that we hoped and more. However something in Ebony's way of performing duties begins to irritate Rodney. No big deal, it isn't all that big of a thing, so nothing is said, but the small issue festers. Like the splinter that only gets worse if not dealt with, things get tense. Everyone of course, knows about the issue - the partner, family, friends, etc.

Everyone except for Ebony of course! Blake subconsciously believes it will just take care of itself, so Blake does nothing. More days and weeks go by and this boss and employee relationship erodes. Slowly, but predictably, communication becomes challenging, avoiding talking happens, etc. We've all been there done that in some way haven't we? Ebony is feeling a bit uneasy but just assumes that if something were really wrong, surely the boss would tell her! Blake and the partner converse about it and continue to be frustrated, and start thinking 'well let's give her a couple of weeks and if nothing changes, well....'

With no performance evaluation or feedback on the issue, it comes to a head of course. One day Ebony makes a mistake totally disconnected with the previous issue, and Blake jumps on her big time for this error. Ebony is upset and has no clue why this was such a big deal ...yeah she made a mistake but did it necessitate all this ranting and raving? Two months and three days from the day she was hired, Ebony is let go. Bad feelings are felt on both sides. Oh well, Blake thinks, 'it's just hard to find good help these days...' Maybe the next one will work out." Janelle pauses sitting back down with lots of heads shaking and grumbling about how stupid that is, but it does happen, and other such remarks.

"I'm almost done guys. My coach, to further emphasize the point to me, shared--across town, a large company with hundreds of employees ...the HR Manager has just hired a new employee after several weeks of interviewing prospects. The new hire works out fine for a while, but is let go about five months in. Nothing different here except the corporation has the budget to do a lot more elaborate assessing and profiling before hiring the *right person* the next time! Supervisor and HR Manager look at each other, shaking their heads and muttering how difficult it is to find good people! It appears TURNOVER is alive and well here in corporate America as well."

Janelle stopped, sipping her huge jug of something she carried around; waiting for reactions. The facilitator took advantage of his need to continue sharing some other points, "Janelle, thanks so much. You have really put the focus where it needs to be. Nice tie in, ..those are some of the practical dynamics and real outcomes that come from a lack of real evaluation and assessment. Thanks really for sharing that."

Debra wanted to get back to the previous conversation, "I really like this ETA concept, and that was a big eye opener Janelle, you really opened my eyes about some areas I need to improve. Turnover is probably my biggest performance flaw as a manager.

So this ETA thing, I really want to get a grip on this. This makes so much sense, as I see it the first piece is expectations; the beginning and yet, more often than not, ends up being the ending that leads back to the beginning. What did I just say? Hang on guys, please let me work this through. I'm not sure what I just said either! Let me try putting it this way instead. In the working relationship between a leader and his/her people, expectations is where much time should and needs to be spent—but oftentimes is not. And ohhhh how we pay for it when we assume rather than spend the time communicating and clarifying what is expected. Both parties need to make sure that this time is committed to....pay me now or pay me later. What is the expected outcome? What is the standard? How much authority is granted? What are the milestones or deadlines? Is there a need for coaching and feedback sessions as we go? How will we measure success? How much experience and capability does the individual possess?

Oh my gosh, it just hit me why I am making numerous calls back to the plant demonstrating a lack of trust by dogging my project manager! I am a micro-manager. I guess the positive here is that now I know how to fix it, I think.

So, am I good here now, am I on track guys?" Debra shifted looking around at those behind her.

"I say absolutely", Belinda from the vicinity of San Diego, CA said. "The trust part is what I want to make sure I am clear on, so let me try it, if that's okay with all?" Not really pausing she went on, "So once the expectations are indeed established, clarified and agreed upon; trust becomes a significant player in the process. There are trust dynamics with both parties that need to be understood, discussed and practiced. Trust is developed in both directions when expectations are clear, feedback is open and we accomplish the tasks at hand. But trust can be stressed and ruined depending on how both leader and follower behave during the process, during the journey. I am thinking how I mess this up, ... the leader, me, ...I violate it when I constantly check, watch, micromanage, question the status, look over their shoulder, and so on.

The follower breaks the trust, which I reckon we all have done by not completing it, and possibly worse than that, bringing it to the boss two minutes prior to deadline stating that they, we cannot get it done. And maaaaannn, is the follower getting ready to be held accountable!

Now the leader, the boss, is on the hook and ultimately responsible and there is no way out for the boss to.... Well yeah, so things turn ugly, and what's the result? Trust and the working relationship is severely eroded regarding future efforts, overall work and situations that arise.

Oh my gosh..." Belinda stood up to go lean against the wall and see everyone better.

"Since we're passing this around, let me do the accountability step, which if I'm being honest here, I would say is my weakness with all this. I try to be too nice and not wanting to be confrontational, I don't hold folks accountable like I should always. And I know it drives everyone else crazy and likely causes them some disrespect in me, ...because I guess it is my job?" Denise from Lenexa, Kansas was embarassingly peering around as she continued.

"Well anyway, I need to process this out loud for me, if you all will allow. This phase or last step can be either good or bad depending on the outcome. I can hold them accountable by chewing their butt, or...praising their good job, ...recognizing failure and ensuring we learn from it, ...or whatever. Typically as I am realizing just now, when things go bad - it all leads back to a lack of time spent on the front end on expectations; and probably some within the trust aspect as well."

The facilitator picked it up from there, "Yes, there must be clarity on the front end, open, honest relevant words regarding this delegation or assignment of duties. Was the follower comfortable enough to ask questions in the initial phase or along the way? Was the leader available? Did we provide him/her with the authority to get it done? Important and necessary questions. Are you guys also seeing how the concepts covered in your previous breakouts tie in here? How and why relationship is important up front. How creating a non threatening environment is essential, and all that?

You guys are all over this ETA thing. Indeed if leaders practice ETA, correctly and effectively, the result will likely turn out in a very expected manner. It doesn't mean we won't fail; but we will learn and this is important, ...we maintain the working relationship!"

The facilitator needing to share a bit more before the session ended; he kept going, "Going back to the annual performance process, let me share something we here think is something worth considering. It is just something that might be a good idea; tell me what you think? What if, after those first couple of meetings, like in February and March possibly, after the discussion is completed you wad up the paper, the agreement form and throw it in the trash can! The point here obviously is to symbolically demonstrate to them that this doesn't matter; actually none do until December! We are focusing on a continuous improvement journey with him or her; just like we are doing with our operations and systems. What do you think?"

There was a good follow up discussion on the idea; most really liked the idea of throwing it away. There were observations and questions about keeping a recorded copy for CYA reasons. There wasn't any real consensus; just something all agreed was a worthwhile consideration.

There followed a discussion of other performance assessment complaints, experiences and ideas. After a few minutes when it was really leaning toward a belly-aching dialogue, the facilitator halted things. As the last facilitator had, and all the others would, the Connections sheets were passed around, as Jack and a couple others actually led most of the discussion.

Evaluate: Great 8 Connections & 'food for thought'...

Notice how the other seven concepts support, reinforce, and connect with this one.

CREATE ...new ways of assessing, measuring, and critiquing people and processes.

ELIMINATE ...evaluation and feedback as "bad" things—ineffectiveness is unacceptable.

FACILITATE ...all evaluating, done by everyone, 360 degrees—including self.

ACCOMMODATE ...new approaches to measuring, reviewing, and improving success

DEMONSTRATE ...self improvement and learning. Never miss monthly discussions and input.

COMMUNICATE ...in an open, direct, and tactful manner—we are accountable for how we address others.

RELATE ...strong relationships enable effective, real and productive assessments.

Please make your own notes and comments below.

"I can't believe it but our time is up gang, I can't even throw in a couple of gems I wanted to share, bummer!" the facilitator clicked the remote to show a quote as all began to move toward the door.

Without Direction, We Wander

"If your actions inspire others to dream more, learn more, do more, and become more, you are a leader."

John Quincy Adams

Debra had always thought she was a great judge of character, so some of today's lessons forced her to start looking at situations that hadn't gone as well as they could have. As part of the 'Know Self' concept, she kept coming back to the questions of what she could do better. Her inner voice was telling her that she didn't do a great job of setting expectations with her team. And her monthly one-on-one performance coaching sessions with staff were painfully awkward and blown off now and then for sure.

She started thinking about her approach to the whole performance review process and how the mixed reactions of her team over the years might be a good indicator that people didn't really understand on just what they were being evaluated.

She was debating the ideas in her mind, and thought back to the example from the discussion about Ebony being initially perceived as very good and subsequently terminated. Debra thought of her own company and how many people had been hired and were either fired or stopped coming to work very quickly. She realized she was guilty of this *Blake* thing.

Was it because I wasn't doing a good enough job with setting expectations? What is this costing me? And what is this costing the company?

She quickly started jotting down the high level process steps and in hiring replacement staff so she had a true idea of the costs.

Debra's Notes about ROI after Breakout #3

Human Resources: Advertise open position, screen applicants, coordinate interviews, extend offers, and complete new hire paperwork. Hours needed per new employee hired to complete those tasks: 10 to 20.

The HR manager had been a pain, extremely vocal about how much work it took to bring on new staff and also made critical comments about how long a new person stayed....or didn't. Is this a leadership issue I need to work on?

Departmental Training: 40 hours of classroom training.

On-the-job Training: 80 hours over the course of the first month working with an experienced Subject Matter Expert (SME) in order to get the person productive and knowledgeable enough to work alone.

(10 to 20) + (40+80) = 130-140 paid hours invested in new employees! I didn't realize—this is amazing! I knew that new employee turnover was expensive, but I'd never really thought too much about it. Instead, I focused on what I *thought* was most important—*production*.

What if I slowed down attrition? How much would that actually impact our production and quality by reducing defects and service impacts? Dang, this could be huge!

Am I constantly managing emergencies, fires, and every crisis that comes along because my team isn't capable? Would I have more quality time both professionally and personally if I trusted them to handle things? Would people wind up being more involved and solve their own problems? Would that impact turnover?

How can I make the team better? I wonder if I followed this ETA model and put it into practice—mentoring and coaching as well as really using the performance appraisal process effectively every month—would the company benefit? Would my department benefit—and my personal life? The numbers keep hitting me.

The amount of staff turnover quarterly, or (x), multiplied by 130 to 140 paid hours of new employee training = a staggering number! Yikes! What am I doing to myself? However you compute turnover, it's killing us. I need to talk to less and the HR manager ASAP—we have to address this right away.

Please use this page for notes.

Breakout Session #4: Create

The facilitator, a native born Mexican, now proud U.S. citizen, named Raul introduced the *Create* breakout session; including a really stupid joke. It was something about why a Mexican chicken crossed the road, ...something like to get away from the Enchilada stand, I don't know.

Some introductory thoughts were along the lines of creating a culture. Raul finished sharing a story personal about him, "It was a cultural bias thing toward me. It was really bad until I had a leader come in and well, fix it. Previously the manager had just deflected bias, jokes, diversity issues, conflict and all to the HR guy to resolve. Nothing ever got resolved; we just did HR classes on sexual harassment, diversity, and you well you get it?

Well this leader came in and broke down these lines, no magical way I could see she did it; it was just that he saw it as his job. I am just a bit believing that women make better leaders in some situations, at least for my situation there. She was persistent and committed to the team concept; and relationships were paramount. I must tell you amigos, it worked; it's where I came to really believe in the team thing for the first time. It was also where I saw the difference maker that leadership really can provide. Those who saw me and my nationality as an issue were just ignorant; I don't mean that badly. By definition, ignorance is just about well, *not knowing*. It had been that way around that community and that company for a long time. I tell you I developed really good relationships with many there; in particular one guy and another lady I still know very well. To be honest with you, the lady I ended up marrying!"

Before he could continue the entire group started cheering, one lady's eyes welled up with tears as she shared a story which all very much connected with, similar to Raul's actually. It just set a great tone for the rest of the session.

The best dressed guy threw in here, "This ties back into what I believe it was the lady from Arkansas was speaking of earlier, I think to get a culture all about team, you better get all having the same vision. I have been thinking what Kenisha said earlier and that makes so much sense. From day one, the leader needs to get all defining what a team is, what it would look like, what behaviors would be good and bad, etc. Then the leader and slowly everybody, holds everybody accountable for those behaviors which builds a real high powered team. Likely some of what your leader back then did, right Raul?"

Raul acknowledged, and there followed various points made about previous break out session topics that connected here. Trust, creating a non-threatening environment, upward communication, relationships, and so on …these were all mentioned again. Raul reinforced something said by all facilitators so far, "You see, I am telling you now for probably the fourth time, that all of these leadership dynamics, the eight concepts are big time overlapping!"

Yolanda, always sitting centered in the back row raised her hand and all quieted, "I would like to spend some time on this Change thing. This isn't exactly probably what was intended here, but I would like to share something. I haven't really said anything much until now, but it seems we right here, are becoming a team", she said smiling and seeing smiles returned. "I trust you all, feel comfortable with the group; and really appreciate Raul sharing his story by the way. Raul, my being a black female from Memphis, I can tell you I experienced some of the same for sure when I married and moved to Ohio several years back.

I am sure you all can guess what that looked like. Anyway, I want to share my story which does connect here I think. I see change being first and foremost hugely tied to individual development and then team development."

All twisted around to see and to listen as Yolanda went on, "Several years back, I had personally gone through many changes in my life to include the move I mentioned; people had come and gone for a variety of reasons. Because of these changes, I had become conscious of a void that had resulted; not having people around to give me honest input, coaching and outside perspective about me. Not just friends but relations that helped me grow and see myself better. I was reading a lot on leadership and self-development at the time; mentoring was something that made sense, so I was looking. Quite by chance I stumbled into the path of someone who became a friend, and had taken up some of that slack and was helping me. It took some boldness on her part, but habits, behaviors, grammar, cultural language issues, jargon, etc needed addressing. Just so you don't think this is just about me rambling on about my life, let me make a couple of quick points and I'll shut up. As I was receiving this input, I had a few choices to make. I could get mad at these things I was hearing about me; I could change the subject, forgive and forget, reject the input as though it wasn't true; ...or I could thank this person for their input."

Raul cut her off, "Yolanda if I may, a quick point. Now think about teams and people on them that we lead; consider what you typically observe when people, or maybe even you, receive feedback or criticism. I agree with what you are thinking - the receiver typically has just had their day ruined! This is a change in people's heads we must change, we as leaders need to create this change. See there's that create thing."

Yolanda picked up as Raul looked back at her, "Precisely Raul; the point is that these observations were right on; just a few little quirks or habits that I had developed unconsciously that could be easily corrected. The only negative takeaway for me is thinking about how many people have written me off or thought less of me because of these quirks, flaws or habits? Why didn't they tell me right then and there? You and I know the answer: they didn't feel comfortable enough, the relationship wasn't strong enough or they didn't want to hurt my feelings, right? The reality here takes us back to the original point: that we all need people in our lives that will do that for us; not *to* us, but *for* us."

Debra slipped into the dialogue just then, getting a nod from Yolanda it was alright, "We heard this earlier, but we are creators in a sense. We need to create or maybe re-create ourselves; and we need to create visions, processes, systems and that culture thing? I am sure the first step is about us, as we heard earlier.

Do we think we are a completed project? Do you think you cannot improve? Do we really want to know our flaws? First of all we must be open to fixing us, re-creating us. This conference's beginning has already stressed that and I am thankful. I was one of those who thought they didn't need to be here. I was one of those who thought I had arrived, if I'm being honest, ...dang it."

Raul responded as Debra twisted and crossed her arms as if frustrated with something, maybe herself. "Leaders help people and ask for help...AND...Leaders seek out mentors as well as mentor others themselves. My recent experience tells me that we had better have those who will point out what needs to be pointed out. This goes for leaders, as well as all of us. Lastly, it is our job to mentor, coach and help others improve; and then to get the team to do it with each other."

That lady next to Debra sighed getting people's attention, then opened up, "I found it interesting that Change was part of this Create session; I knew it would be part of this conference and actually seemed to fit in other places. As I was sitting here listening to Yolanda blab on.... just kidding my friend. You actually did a great job getting me to think of how everything is about change. Leadership development is about change; we are about change if we are here for the right reasons; and we really need to understand change deeply and personally in order to facilitate it with our teams it seems. Effective teams must be led by leaders who can facilitate change effectively and that's not easy. Teams that can change effectively are the ones that will kick butt."

Raul took the lead again, "So anyway, I want to share with you some dynamics that we believe in and preach about around here.

First of all, we all know it's a fact of life that all organizations and all of our teams must deal with changes. Think about how most people, maybe even you typically respond to this question: Why do people react negatively to change? The typical/normal dribble answer is 'blah, blah, blah....people just resist change naturally.'

I used to say the same thing, but now I say pardon my French, but that's just crap, management crap. It's the stuff managers who don't know how to lead change ...think about change!

Here's our take and what I personally think for sure. People resist change for very good reasons, life experience and valid rationalizations. Let's take into consideration these three factors...

First, people perceive that we are *trying to change them* vs. the continuous improvement process...

Second, people don't like to be *surprised*; the surprise factor...

And third, people *having no part* in the development of the change.

Yolanda jumped in, "Raul, I really like that. If you don't mind, I am taking this back and see if I can convey this as well as you maybe, amigo!

This really is a great way of explaining it. It's so real. People will take it as you trying to change them. People really have no other choice, you see, they are part of that process for the moment until someone new moves into that role, which may happen because of the reaction you are likely to get from them in response. Most will be unable to separate themselves from the improvement of a process; unless it is carefully communicated to them. And, oh yeah, that would have happened except that we forgot to consult and involve them and therefore the change came as a big surprise which we want them to just blindly accept and begin doing tomorrow morning! How did I do Raul?"

Alicia took the lead before he could say anything; as all acknowledged agreement, "The surprise factor is so what we do to people. I'm thinking what we do in the normal evolution of a change in our organization? See if this has a familiar ring to it? At some level an idea starts to brew...management takes charge...meetings begin to occur...lots of discussion, listening, reasoning, and understanding of the different points of view. Of course, only the management types attend these meetings because we cannot interrupt production, services, daily operations, etc. Slowly, *we*, management, begin to digest the idea or change; it is accepted by all the key players and a decision is born...maybe over weeks, months, etc. Now it is time to take it to the floor and see what they think, like it really matters at this point, right?"

"Oh, my gosh! That is exactly what we do in our company," blurted Jack in the back; also many were nodding as well. "And with this ownership thing, what's happening here? We've brought this to you, the employees and it's a great idea! We suggest to them, to trust us, we have thought this through from every possible angle ...it's the best thing since sliced bread. It *will* work, now go do it!

I can tell you from personal painful experience, it may work, but only after a whole lot of wasted time, stress, arguing, hammering each other, ...maybe each other's mothers, hurt feelings, damaged relations, explaining, and so on. The almost comical part of this as I think about it is that it might have indeed been a very good idea. The way we implemented it made it needlessly painful. Thus people naturally resist change; you're right, there is nothing natural about it. Leaders do this to people; place this resistance in their heads, their hearts."

Raul smiling interjected, "You guys are super, you hit it all pretty well I think. As you think of this all happening to people all their lives in different parts of their lives from parents, to teachers, bosses, other role models, etc; as Jack said just then ...it probably wasn't natural. It was a negative attitude developed about change that was really just painful learning that happened for all of us over a lifetime. We didn't come out of the womb that way; we were taught that resistance over time weren't we?"

The lady next to Debra very quietly shared, "When will we ever learn these lessons and stop doing it to our people? When will we quit doing it to the organization over and over again? I guess when we do; these common phrases and words will finally be silenced, to be heard no more. Things like, '...Boy, people these days just don't accept change very well do they? ...or people just naturally resist change, nothing you can do about it!' We are the leaders and do such stupid stuff."

Raul coughing, clearing his throat to get attention, realizing time was getting short, "Now here's another way of putting it maybe, people haven't changed much, they've always wanted to know why and be involved. Didn't you, didn't all of us?" he was smiling and taking a few follow up comments, as he was running very short and needed to wrap up things.

"Did anyone have any thought as to what the last bullet there about fate might mean?" Raul waited for any response. Seeing no one jumping in on this one, "No big deal, it is just to wrap up and say that leaders either create the team, create processes, create everywhere, or leave all this to fate. I think by the way, the vast majority just leave it all to fate. That fate approach is why likely society and most workplaces possess a dim view of management and managers, huh? Managers maintain, and maybe maintaining what is there is exactly that, leaving everything to fate. I'll leave you to work on that since we're short on time anyway."

Debra, somewhat embarrassed, cut in with, "Raul this doesn't fit exactly with what you just asked or said, maybe not at all. But still I wanted to share another neat thing I picked up a couple of months back. It was something someone sent to me they got off their email. It was about trust. It was a sort of definition and it so fits into another one of those impacts on building a team. It went something like trust defined is the knowledge that you will not deliberately or consciously take unfair advantage of me. I can put my situation, problems, opinions and self-esteem in your hands with confidence. Loyalty to each other is highly valued and is a top priority to each of us. I am just thinking if we all took that to heart, we would do so much of this leadership stuff better, and with people, not to them. I'm done now."

Debra looked down and began collecting her materials as she said, "No no, no. No need to apologize my friend that was good, very good. I like that and going to write it down here before we move on."

Raul added on immediately, "I am writing that down quickly also, as soon as you all vamoose, scram; you have got to go. But before you do go, let's go through the Connections sheet, and see if we can further clarify the principle's relationships with each other." The best dialogue thus far occurred as they uncovered some amazing dynamics connecting the principles, four of them very thoroughly understood.

Create: Great 8 Connections & 'food for thought'...

Notice how the other seven concepts support, reinforce, and connect with this one.

ELIMINATE ...barriers to new ideas, creativity, and imagination of new approaches.

FACILITATE ...brainstorming, problem solving, decision making, and new players.

ACCOMMODATE ...new and different approaches, relations, reasoning, and logic.

DEMONSTRATE ...open-mindedness, receptiveness to opposing ideas.

COMMUNICATE ...pass on and facilitate information, ideas, and approaches.

RELATE ...connect players, information, systems, and operations.

EVALUATE ...constantly assess and measure old ways of doing things and new solutions and ideas.

Please make your own notes and comments below.

"Your first day is done!" Raul announced, "but I'll be here for a bit if anyone wants to hang around and talk about, oh, I don't know....maybe some leadership stuff! In fact all of the facilitators will be here for the next hour." He was smiling hugely as he added, "Oh, yeah, and here's something to leave you with..." as he clicked the remote:

> Managers maintain what's already there.
>
> Leaders improve, grow, create, and make stuff (and people!) better.
>
> Managin' ain't Leadin'!

Debra had no illusion as to how many people on her team she could trust. While she liked the thought on the culture of team she didn't really think the concept applied to her. Then the thought crossed her mind how much the lack of trust was costing her and maybe even the company.

How many extra hours and effort was required due to her not being able to trust her team. I tell them what to do but somehow cannot get them to do it without me demanding and checking... This was a thought she had so many times during a normal day she couldn't keep track.

Her mind flashed back to the last slide Raul had put up, 'Managers maintain what is there'. She smiled wistfully as she looked back up at the wall, staring at it for a bit.

Debra's Notes about ROI after Breakout #4

It takes all of my time, effort, energy, and emotional fortitude to "maintain" production. How can I become the leader who can "improve, grow, create, and make better"?

I can't trust my team. What are some ways to make the group improve? What if I had more people I could trust? I could spend more time focusing on improvement. If the team had trust in each other, it would be because they trusted me. Now that's a sobering thought! I have to do it first.

My team doesn't trust me. That's because I don't have a team, I have a bunch of employees. (I'm sitting here consciously uncomfortable thinking about all of this.) What if I—scratch that thought—what if we could work together with trust and a clear set of defined and measurable objectives with a shared burden and reward for our team? We can make significant, dramatic improvements.

Like most people, I prefer the sound of the word "we" rather than the word "I." It is empowering and intoxicating as the possibilities are running through my mind. I can ENVISION it myself and then I must create that vision within my team.

My pragmatic mind and habits lead me to calculate the benefits of these possible improvements. What about efficiency, process improvements, enhancements to existing systems and tools? What about production, quality, turnover, and overtime, which are all part of the initial equations? Even being conservative here, I can see that when we ALL work together as a team with trust and respect, focused on improving the business,

....we should expect at least a 3 to 5% improvement in operational effectiveness through reduced costs, better processes, enhancements, and overall organizational efficiency.

Please use this page for notes.

Day one of the conference was over. There were conversations going on between attendees and every one of the facilitators. Book sales, networking and evening coordination's were happening; plenty of folks were simply rushing out the doors to soak up the beautiful weather and bright sunshine.

David Parker, another local small business owner invited was doing the meet and greet thing, helping people with directions and information. David is another community leader and former graduate student of Booker's. He is now operating his own business, and was handing out business cards. He was smiling and carrying on in a loud voice about how it doesn't get any better than this ...the weather, the learning and being in Kansas City!

Parker Business Change Solutions
Kansas City, MO 64188
(816) 582-4175

Web site: Parkerbcs.com
Email: David@Parkerbcs.com

"When leaders change, organizations change"

Debra had headed back to her room to clean up after she and Les had some discussions. Both had been totally pleased so far and had agreed there was much here for them to take back to the CEO and TBI. Les found a seat on a bench out in the brightness of the day; only minutes passed before the bus from Lexington with Mickey pulled up in front of the Sprint Center front doors.

Mickey was wound up talking a hundred miles an hour about some people she met on the bus; the scenic route they had taken along the Missouri River and how beautiful everything was in Lexington. She carried on about the beautiful County Courthouse with a cannonball in a pillar from the Civil War battle fought there in the area. They had met the mayor and chamber director; and ate at a tea room of some sort in the heart of the town. They had gone through lots of shops and taken a tour on a trolley through the streets. She told him about gorgeous historic homes, pretty old trees and the huge flower pots on corners throughout downtown.

They both were really leaning now toward staying on and touring around a bit, and catching that Beatles concert Monday night. They strolled and talked as they made their way back to their room.

Mickey checked in with Jackson, checking on the dog and all, while Les plopped on the bed shutting his eyes for a few moments. The call ended and after Mickey updated Les on the issues back home, she too fell on the bed cuddling up next to her husband. It wasn't long before Les became a bit frisky, and after a few attempts to get him to stop, they both agreed to go experience the double-headed spacious shower. A very nice ending to the afternoon's events, ...definitely!

The Evening Social and Speech *(optional):*
"God Knows Leadership"

Dinner was outstanding. The Power & Light District and this place were hits with all in attendance. Plates had been taken away, coffee had been served; some were still picking at their desert. Seeing the Master of Ceremony (MC) moving toward the stage, everyone twisted in their seats or moved their chairs completely around to face the stage.

Raul, one of the breakout facilitators and tonight's MC broke in, "Hope dinner was satisfactory?" He paused knowing he would get plenty of acknowledgements and agreement to that question. "We have a bit of a change with our evening. Pastor Emmanuel, who was to be our speaker, has suffered some kind of serious health issue, we aren't sure yet, maybe even a heart attack. We don't know all the details, but please keep him in your prayers. Sorry for the change, but being leaders, we are sure you can handle change, right?

We are also sure you will not be disappointed with his stand-in. He is someone you have already met and well, from personal experience, I can assure you will indeed enjoy the message. I will just stop and turn it over to my own boss and friend, Booker!"

All began to applaud and looked to the right seeing him step up to the stage and begin walking across. He waved to them smiling big as usual. As he closed in on the podium, the house lights gradually dimmed. The petite candles on the tables and shadow lights on the walls created a pretty cool ambience. He placed his finger to his lips, "shhhhhh..."

As the applause settled and quiet became the only sound, he stood completely motionless and began, "He awakened, this close friend of mine, shivering even though covered by two or three blankets. These were some very tough times for him. Life had bottomed out, he had very little money, a wardrobe pretty much completely from the Thrift stores he routined, skipping meals to save money for gas, etc.

Anyway, it was middle of the night, and he was in a run-down concrete fishing cabin on Table Rock Lake in central Missouri. It wasn't much due to his current lot in life, but it was home temporarily; the most he could afford. It was late October, nearly Halloween, with winter approaching. It was going to be a hard winter; a fair amount of snow had already fallen that month. As it turned out, he would be stranded much of that winter in this little place in the Ozarks. He would discover before this season was over, this might not be such a bad thing in some ways.

Yes, cold weather was settling in, and he was driving this piece of junk pickup truck with four bald tires. The cabin sat in a deep valley in a southern fork on the lake; very few people remained there over the cold weather months. The cabin had little heat, except for a fireplace and a couple of cheap space-heaters he had picked up at the Salvation Army store. My friend was one of those who actually loved the whole outdoors scene......fireplace, hauling wood, cutting wood and all that he enjoyed. He had a love of the outdoors, wintertime, birds and critters; sitting by the fireplace and all that sort of thing. It was kind of a neat setting, even if he was flat broke with little idea how he would ever recover. The cabin set by the lake shore maybe only fifty meters away. This was a cool situation he figured. *Cool* really didn't describe what it turned out to be there, it was downright cold; he would tell you that if he were here!

Keeping wood on that fire day and night was important. I can still picture his description; he would go to bed with a stocking cap and lots of clothes on and covered up with anything he could. He would have to get up at least once most every night to stoke the fire, throw another log on the fire...you get the picture.

Let me tell you right about now he would be telling you that this is not intended to sound like a sob story. This is not a sad story; in fact this story has much more significance to all this than *my....* ah, ahem, I mean *his* struggles and troubles at that time."

Booker stopped and momentarily stepped back from the podium, pausing and staring off. There was an awkward moment of silence with people in the audience looking around questioningly at each other.

Just then, with a grin, he returned to the podium offering, "Alright, I've let the cat out of the bag haven't I? Maybe you were already suspecting it; please forgive me for trying to deceive you. This is actually my own personal story I have been describing. Who I have been talking about was me about a decade ago."

After some laughter, chuckling, applause and amen's, he continued on, "So let me tell you the rest of the story, as ol' Paul Harvey would put it.

This was one of the very worst and yet very best times in my life. On the human side, I had huge struggles happening; but on the God side, well...I had found Him. I had found Jesus you see, I was a new man!" Again, another round of amen's and applause took hold. There was all that, but a respectable silence also settled over the room of maybe 65-70 folks in attendance.

"At least now as I look back, I am very sure it was indeed one of the very best periods of my life," Booker was smiling. "I love to share this story. So much has changed and I have learned so much since those days, and I have been so very blessed....amazingly so.

Anyway, that winter I spent my time engulfed in reading the bible, writing a book I had begun, staying warm, walking along the shoreline, and actually fishing for my meals now and then. I love fishing but for sure not very adept at it I must tell you.

Another interesting thing happened during this period; some serious arthritis had somewhat suddenly settled into my hips. I had for the previous 20 years or so, been big into running, long distance races, marathons, triathlons, and all that sort of thing. Running and exercise was critical to my life, dealing with stress, staying physically in shape, working out, etc. I think to this day, that that...getting arthritis, which shut down my running, was God saying 'no you are not going to run away from *this*'. I really think He wanted me focused on Him and our relationship. Whether that is what was happening or not, I am not sure, but will always believe that He shut me down in that regard. I really felt like an old man, and only in my early 40s! I even bought a cane at one point in there. I had no money to go to the doctor. All is good now - that relationship with Him and my hips as well; I had my hips both replaced in 2006. Just running toward him these days!

Now let me take you backward in time a bit, about nine months prior to that winter. It was somewhere around the year 2000 and I was in the midst of a disastrous marriage, bankruptcy and generally bottoming out in life. For the record, I am indeed now in my last marriage and it is an amazing one. I know that's because the Good Lord is in my life now. He led me to a great Believer and lady, my wife Sydney. She sits right over there", pointing down to his left for people to spot her. She momentarily stood and waved at the audience.

"Anyway, things were really bad, very bad in every regard personally. I had met this insurance salesman, and invited him over to listen to what he had. His name, which I will never forget was Ronnie Black. After just moments sitting at the kitchen table, he revealed he was a minister, as well as an insurance salesman. To this day, I have little doubt that the

Good Lord put Ronnie in my life for a reason. We ended up spending the next hour or so talking about the pain in my life.

Without going into great detail, let me share one thing that he shared with me that was the key to me beginning to understand new things."

Walking over to a large whiteboard Booker had placed off to the left side of the stage, he grabbed a marker and drew a triangle, saying, "Ronnie drew this on a piece of paper, and then placed these words at each point". "YOU and your SPOUSE/PARTNER on the bottom corners of the triangle, and then wrote GOD at the top of the triangle.

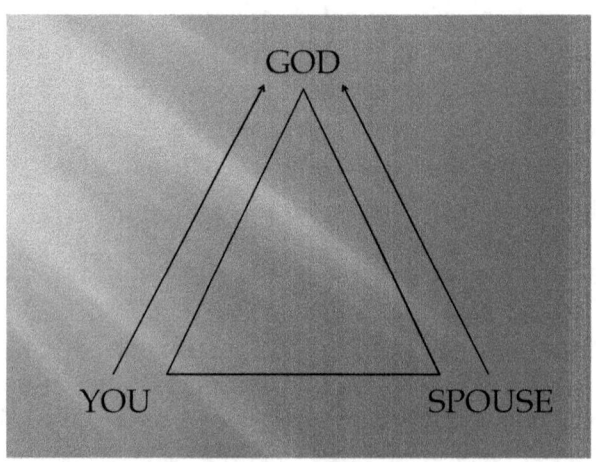

Ronnie went on to explain, "Our first and most important relationship in life for each and every one of us is the one with Him. If first you and your wife or spouse are not both focused and working toward GOD up at the top, then you are just staying apart. If one is moving that way and the other is not, then you are actually growing further away from each other. If both are moving up the triangle toward Him, then you are growing closer together, as you move individually and jointly toward the relationship with God.

Well let me just say, not to draw this out any more than I already have, this diagram just hit me like a ton of bricks. I just knew that's why this marriage and other past relationships had failed. Indeed it was crystal clear why my life was failing on every front. I am not sure how it all works, although I am sure to this day that it was GOD talking, telling me this. What it meant to me was that although I didn't really know much yet, this triangle thing and us both moving in that direction was definitely not happening....and would not happen with this person whom I had married. That's enough about that.

As I remember things, this was the trigger to what all evolved over the next weeks and months....divorce, bankruptcy, nearly losing my kids, plenty of pain, and so forth."

Booker paused for a moment, taking a sip of water placed there at the podium. He wanted to allow all to digest what had been said to this point, as well as just looking for reactions. He continued, after some folks muttered some acknowledgements about how good our God is, what a tough time that must have been and other such thoughts.

"As I mentioned this earlier, and no, I didn't know it at the time, this was the best year of my life up to that point. For the next maybe three to five months I spent a couple of nights a week at Ronnie's home sitting in his office while we explored the WORD, Jesus Christ, what the bible said and God. Well, within that next year or so, I moved many times, from Jonesboro, Arkansas to Memphis, to Table Rock Lake, and more, thus the story I just shared.

Somewhere in the midst of all those talks, discussions and exploring, I finally came to understand, that all *this* was simply about actually believing in the fact that there was a JESUS CHRIST who really did come down to earth and really did die on a cross for our sins. To me, this is the Way and the Truth, what I believe anyway.

I can still vividly remember one evening sitting exploring with Ronnie in his office, when that happened and I got it. I was a Believer and one of those *saved* folks. I was new and asked Jesus to forgive my sins and let me into His Kingdom. This whole *being saved* thing had always seemed weird to me...but it doesn't now.

So, that's enough of my story. Thanks for letting me share it with you.

And now so we can get out of here at some point tonight, let me quickly share what you actually came for tonight, the Reverend's message, titled GOD KNOWS LEADERSHIP.

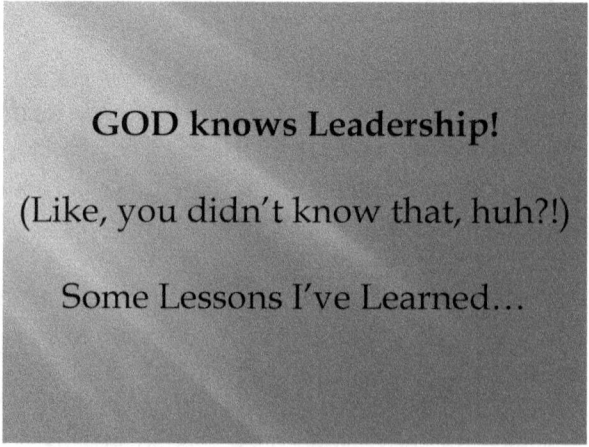

GOD knows Leadership!

(Like, you didn't know that, huh?!)

Some Lessons I've Learned...

Okay, so here are these five ideas that Pastor Immanuel was going to cover with you tonight. That first part was just me taking advantage of you guys and witnessing my story while I had you...pretty sneaky. huh?

This is his stuff, but trust me it's good and powerful. Bear with me and I will try to convey it to you as best I can. I am going to essentially just share this with you straight through, and we'll deal with any questions or thoughts at the end."

He nods to the back of the auditorium for the audio visual person to move to the first slide.

> "...Blessed is the man who finds wisdom; the man who gains understanding."
> PROVERBS 3:13
>
> "...He who loves discipline loves knowledge, he who hates correction is stupid..."
> PROVERBS 12:1

"What is wisdom anyway? As we think of it in regard to leadership, likely many believe it to be centered on how the product(s) is made or how we provide our service(s). Since there are many in management who totally know the product/service, but still struggle in leading their people effectively – doesn't it have to be something more?

Is it just about the business and operational know-how, or could it be something different? I believe it is undoubtedly about all of it - the knowledge of the business, people skills, human behavior/nature, process/systems-thinking, group dynamics and even some organizational development *stuff* thrown in...! Think about it, if you knew about all that and practiced it in your role as a leader, you would likely have to be a pretty amazing leader?

Leaders frequently believe they are *there*, they have arrived. Therefore they must *know it all* ...or at least more than those they lead. If that is so, how do I use that knowledge, that wisdom in leadership? Do I share it, teach it to others, keep it to myself, or just use it to make all the decisions myself?

I always have to be careful in challenging managers, people like all of us here...you guys! Remember, this is not about anyone being bad, but just about bad management and leadership practices maybe.

The scriptures up there encourage us to find and discover wisdom, maybe above anything else. Again, I ask you to consider here, 'what is leadership wisdom; what do leaders need to know'? Hopefully you found some answers today and will find even more of those answers tomorrow.

Along with our own understanding, opinions and beliefs in this matter, we should seek the input of others around us. We should identify; work on our leadership competencies and ask others to help us with our learning journey. We need to be okay with those and their input when they do point out things or challenge us when we are falling short. Wisdom would tell us that old phrase, 'two heads are better than one' is a truism. A lack of wisdom would cause the leader to not ask other's opinions or to reject feedback from others."

Smiling and pausing for a moment to let people think, he looked toward the back for the next slide, "Here's our second point."

> "...Now before the feast of the Passover, when Jesus knew that his hour was come that he should depart out of this world unto the Father; having loved his own which were in the world, he loved them unto the end..."
>
> JOHN 13:1

"There's a lot there isn't there? Some pretty heavy stuff. We hear from many leaders, '...don't get too close to your people. There's a fine line to be kept between you and your people ...keep your distance ...you can't be a friend and a boss.'

These are commonly spoken and widely accepted management myths heard when people speak of the workplace and a manager's relationship with his or her people. Managers say those things maintaining the status quo. Just possibly real leaders know it is just management-speak. The leader grows, builds & improves these relationships and all relations continually! Real leaders know their success depends on the quality of these relationships.

Because so many people have seen this fine line-concept necessary due to past manager's abusing their authority and position; it has come to be accepted in management circles. It is found in management-theory courses and most anyplace you see management taught. However, we here agree with the pastor on this, we don't buy it for a second. We are teaching leadership and relationship here at the Great Eight Conference. You've already witnessed some of that in today's sessions haven't you?

We believe this mentality comes from bad experiences where untrained managers, not leaders practiced favoritism, abused their roles, not holding all equally accountable, taking advantage of people, promoting on friendship, and so on.

If you are a leader or trying to become one, realize this. If your attempts at leadership have been less than productive, very likely this is at the root of your problems.

Your success is going to come from them, your people, and those relationships. What kind of leader would YOU perform for the best? What leader have YOU worked for the most effectively? Of course the answer is the one you had the best relationship with, right? We speak of the importance of relationships among team members and how dysfunctional teams are when relationships aren't good. But then we suggest the leader needs to keep his or her distance? What kind of illogical nonsense is that I ask you?

Don't fall into that way of thinking; work on developing relationships with your folks as tightly as possible. When you create comfort, trust, respect, great communications and a desire for people to want to be there with YOU and the others......great things can and will happen. When you and the team have great relationships all the way around, these are where the good stories come from. The result is awesome productivity, loyalty, low turnover and believe it or not, people looking forward to coming to work ...and maybe even being willing to stay late! When the leader cares about his or her folks ...when the leader is there for them outside their job ...when the leader wants to support, listen and help them with troubles ...and yes even socializes with them ....now we have a great family-like work environment.

Now of course, there are issues and risks to be understood; but not if YOU the leader do things right! If fair expectations and accountability happen with everyone, these issues don't exist! The problem is NOT about this buddy and boss concept and debate; it's about YOU the leader, and your leadership! I have indeed worked with and coached great leaders who would not go there as I am describing! They maintained this fine line and wouldn't let the relationship exist past it. It's just my opinion they were limiting themselves & the potential of this relationship. They were creating a barrier to further good stuff happening. They have created a boundary and limit to any further being achieved as the leader there possibly.

Jesus broke bread and spent countless hours teaching, socializing & continuously improving the relationships with those he led. The Word speaks to developing a personal relationship with HIM. Shouldn't the most ultimate leader's leadership be our guide, think about it?"

Lots of amen's and applause from various parts of the room followed. He allowed for a couple of follow-up comments to be made quickly before giving the nod to the audiovisual technician...

> "…therefore I tell you, do not worry about life, what you will eat or drink; or about your body, what you will wear. Who of you by worrying can add a single hour to his life? O ye of little faith! Your Heavenly Father knows what you need. Seek first His Kingdom and righteousness and all these things will be given to you. Therefore do not worry about tomorrow."
> MATTHEW 6:25-34

"Let's continue on so I can get you folks out of here sometime tonight. Our third point of the pastor's is important guys. Not worrying is a tough concept for all of us humans, no matter who you are! Leaders have to deal with this personally …as well as for those they lead! That's leadership we're talking about here, not managers who think people should leave their worries at the front door!

In these challenging times with so much hurting, hopelessness, bad economy; people, folks losing jobs, business struggling, oil spilling, tornados, tsunamis, earthquakes, disasters here and there, people laid off …who or what is next? Will it be you, a loved one or some of those you lead? It is nearly a daily occurrence to hear from someone close in our lives who have been hit by something negative right? I heard from a good friend and executive just this morning that is now out of a job; then hearing that they just discovered cancer in her body. Problems and concerns are everywhere, and we're not supposed to worry?!? Indeed, this is one of the tougher biblical principles we are supposed to follow… Yikes, I mean double yikes."

Booker paused, grabbing his water for a sip. He then went on, "As leaders we are *really* needed by those we lead. As much as we may want to focus & dwell on our own worries, stresses and problems ...your folks need you and your leadership! A few points to share as I have been pondering this much lately myself, and with my own team here at the conference.

First off, let them know you also have concerns personally, as well as your concern for them. Be human, be real, and don't be afraid of letting them see it. When we let others in ...we build trust and strong relationships. Some believe this shows weakness as a leader, that's not only wrong, but stupid. That's just my opinion, mind you."

"The relationships in our lives make tough times much more palatable; especially when one of those relationships is his or her boss ...our boss even!   When we all get through these times, which we will, unless we don't..." he paused momentarily smiling at all. "Things will turn around, but in the meantime trusting relationships you built with them will pay huge dividends.

Relationships between co-workers can become very strained as individuals withdrawal, focus and concentration dims, and/or people lashing out at others. Don't avoid it or try to pretend stress is not there. It is real and everyone feels it. Why not get it out for all to know and realize that we are all dealing with it. You the leader and the rest of the team are there for each other. It needs to be be dealt with, exposed and curtailed before it gets out of hand. Although we can never be sure of our security (of our jobs) and those that we lead, we need to reassure our people as much as possible; and with the truth as we know it!

You may be thinking that you are not there to be a counselor, therapist or psychologist!   I for one totally disagree. Real leaders are absolutely those things; they are conscious and realize that their job is indeed all of these and more. It may not be in your job description, but trust me, the ones you lead know what they need from you."

Without pause he pointed to the back, to the audiovisual technician, who was way ahead of him.

> "...You have heard, 'Love your neighbor and hate your enemies.' But I tell you, 'Love your enemies and pray for those who persecute you, that you may be sons of your Father in Heaven.' If you love those who love you, what reward will you get? Even the tax collectors do that. And if you greet only your brothers, what are you doing better, or more, than others?..."
>
> MATTHEW 5:43

"Number four here tonight. This scripture has particular significance to all of us in the workplace, just as in every part of our lives. This reminds me of something I wrote a few years ago regarding working with others. The article focused on the challenge of working with those we don't get along with ...those we are in conflict with ...or let's just say the relationship is less than good! Loving those with whom we work can be tough, but we are called to do so. Maybe HE would accept us just *liking* them and getting along with these others?

We all have these people in our lives from time to time. The correct response should be to address them as quickly as possible to get that stress out of our lives. For me, in my leadership preaching and teaching, it is about the insanity of working side by side with a bad relationship

...day after day after day after day. It's like that Groundhog Day movie, out a while back, every morning he woke up and faced exactly the same day, dynamics, relationships, issues, etc. I believe we just become numb and unconscious of the stupidity of this. We lose focus on just how much they are impacting us and those around us, and them."

Leaders are really needed in these situations. We are the ones responsible to be watching for these conflicts, issues and what we refer to around here as bottlenecks.

Yes, the personal leadership of solving these relationships not just in your life, but also those you manage and supervise in the workplace. He, she, they need you to get involved and facilitate real resolution. You are needed to get them out of this insanity, when they can't or won't by themselves.

The reality is that we must deal with these relationships - it is your job! For the record, it is always your business, no matter the circumstances! Why? ...because people in conflict, to some degree have to be negatively impacting productivity, communications, relationships, morale...

How you do it may seem challenging, however the first step is to be committed and persist in not letting them exist on your team. That's what you are paid the big bucks for, isn't it? We'll be giving you some tips and strategies on this in our breakout sessions by the way.
As you begin to hesitate or procrastinate about taking action with any of this; remember that HE, as in Matthew 5:43, up there on the wall ...directs us to do so."

He was smiling at them with an inquisitive look on his face and nodding for the last time for his last slide.

> "When they saw Jesus having dinners
> with tax collectors and 'sinners,' they
> asked his disciples, 'Why does your
> teacher eat with them'? On hearing
> this, Jesus said, 'It is not the healthy
> who need a doctor, but the sick. Go and
> learn what this means....
> For I have not come for the righteous,
> but sinners and the sick.'"
> MATTHEW 9:11-13

"So here's the last one for tonight. There are so many messages within these scriptures up here, for leaders. Allow me to focus on one I relate to a lot, one I use in discussions with leaders. First off, here's an assumption from my first book if I may...

'Both leaders and followers in the workplace and our society have become accepting and numb to ineffective leadership. Most of us have accepted how non-productive, unenthusiastic, and ineffective management and our quote teams ...and those around us really are! We accept this as just the way it is and poor relationships between individuals and departments, conflicts and bottlenecks, poor attitudes, bad apples and bad management, ...are just part of the landscape'.

The point I make a lot is regarding this *bad-apples* thought. There is this conscious or subconscious thinking on the part of many in leadership roles, ...that there just will always be a couple of bad apples on any team. These bad apples might be viewed as the two or three folks on every team that have issues, life problems, ...they cause trouble, ... they challenge you and others all the time, ...don't seem to be team-players, ...

the ones always in conflict,... or some other shortcoming. You are picturing someone right now aren't you?" Booker smiled, actually strolling across the stage to the other side, then continuing on.

"In looking back at the scripture, Jesus speaks of HIS role to teach, serve lead, heal and teach!   The righteous or healthy ones, the other eighty percent or whatever of those on your team, are not who need your leadership. It's the bad apples. Leaders tend to take credit for the eighty percent, and use the bad-apple excuse to avoid their job as the leader ...there is where the real leadership challenge is. Likely the other eighty just really require any ol' knucklehead manager!

Managers & organizations often just view these bad apples as if they are unsalvageable; the only solution is to just get rid of them. While there is undoubtedly a small percentage that deserve this and need to be tossed out, ...the vast majority in my humble opinion, can be led to become healthy productive team players.

Are you up for your leadership challenge, to go back and fix those bad apples you have been using as an excuse? Are you willing to have dinners with the sick, those in need; to teach and make them well? Jesus knew his purpose. Do you, do we, and does organizational leadership get this ...not many I'd say. What say you?"

Booker was headed back to the podium, grabbed his water, acknowledged a few commentaries and offered, "That's it, some pretty good food for thought I'd say. I hope you find it ties in with all your learning today and tomorrow. We better get out of here gang. I want you fresh for some more learning tomorrow. Don't forget, if interested we have a short church service planned in the morning. If you didn't know or you want some information, check with us on the way out of here. Go enjoy a nice stroll back to the hotel in the great Kansas City weather going on out there."

People were beginning to rise and applauding enthusiastically. He excitedly motioned for them to stop, which they did after a few moments.

Most remained standing, turning back toward Booker. "Thank you for that. Before we go, let me end this with a challenge to you to share *your* story with others! This is not a matter of imposing on others. We are charged to witness to others, to bring others to know about our God. So as I have done with you tonight, you are accountable to start sharing yours. Now, that's obviously up to each one of us. God's very best to each of you, thanks again for coming tonight. I'll be around here for a bit and of course all day tomorrow at the conference. Don't forget church in the morning if interested." All again rose and clapped as he clicked off the podium light, gathered his notes and bottle of water, heading down the stairs to mingle. He did so until nearly 11:15 pm that night.

Please use this page for notes.

Walking Home from the Evening's Events

Debra left Mickey and Les about halfway home on their walk afterward. She was thinking hard on a lot of things and besides wanted to give Mickey and Les some alone time. They didn't say anything, but...

She sat down on a bench, looking up at all the stars soaking up a beautiful evening. She grabbed her little notebook from her purse, quickly jotting down some thoughts:

<u>God Talk, Leader Conference, Kansas City</u>

Tell stories, my faith, teach, and preach—and listen.

Bad apples—have I given up on them?

Help them with stress and personal problems—be there for them.

My attitude: Be okay with being wrong. Tough one!

Be committed and persistent. ALL conflicts can be fixed—really!

Set up some outings with the team.

PRAY—myself, and maybe with the team???

Les, Mickey, and Debra met in the lobby Sunday morning at 6am; attending the church service the conference had put together. With people missing church, they invited a local minister in to serve those interested. Even though several people commented about attending, it did not appear that there were as many as Debra expected.

Debra, Les and Mickey continued with small talk until nearly the time for service to start. In the conference room marked Salon D were set about 120 chairs in what appeared to be a single aisled maze throughout the room. "More like a labyrinth, " Debra said to herself as she peered into the room. Certain paths were blocked by walls or opposite facing chairs.

She leaned over to Mickey "I'm going to visit the restroom before we get started". On the way to the restroom, a young African American man in jeans and a sport coat interrupts Debra's brisk scamper to facilities. Although casual, he seemed to have a slightly fatigued look to his slightly unshaved face. The bald man pushed up his glasses and said for what must have been the second time based on his tone "Miss???" Debra stopped, responding, "Yes?""

He said to her, "You dropped it... is that a pointer or something?" Debra looked in the direction that the man was gesturing and saw a silver cylinder.

Debra assumed it was one of the pens she picked up from the meetings yesterday, even though it did not look familiar. As she stood still gazing at the object on the floor, the man said "better grab it before someone rolls their way to the hospital on it'". She shrugged and decided that it did not matter if it were hers or not – she simply needed to get to the ladies room and return, quickly – or getting up this early was pointless. Grabbing the silver cylinder from the floor and putting it hastily in the side of her purse, she said, "Of course, and thanks and good morning by the way," and proceeded to her private destination.

As Debra returned to Salon D, she noticed that the attendance changed dramatically in only a few quick moments. The room that was nearly vacant, now had very little room – maybe only ten seats remained. She hurriedly found Les and Mickey and scurried over to the empty space next to them – in the middle of the collage of chairs.

Les was intrigued to attend the sermon from Pastor Chauncey Dixon, as he had heard of this pastor who was overseeing a ministry he founded in Merriam, KS but also a 120 year old church in Bonner Springs, KS called First Baptist Church.

"Good morning, everyone! Good morning!" Mickey wonders where the voice is coming from because no one was on the stage. "Wow! So good to see all of you this morning! I know you have had a lot of information given to you and of course, I had the pleasure of sitting in on a few of your sessions – even the one last night – and I will tell you, you all have had some wonderful teaching and training. Debra's was surprised to realize the man speaking was the bald, fatigued looking black man she had run into out in the hallway. She then looked in the side pocket of her purse and took out the cylinder – on the top section of the cylinder it read 'You never know when you will need your light'. She twisted the cylinder and realized it was not a pointer or a pen; it was indeed a flash light.

"Before we begin, let us bow our heads in a word of prayer... Our Father and our Lord, we thank you for another opportunity simply to come into your presence in worship. We honor you today and we pray that you would grant us understanding of principle so that we can influence lives and hearts, even beyond our own. We love you and give your name all of the glory and honor that is due your name... Amen.

Today instead of a traditional sermon, I want to share with you a few thoughts from the Word of God and hopefully provoke your mind to consider that if you were made in the image of God, somewhere – down deep inside of you – there is a light in you to help you in leading the way that God desires. God Himself is the perfect leader, the most incredible manager the world has ever known! God is the light and He is your guide to true leadership.

Now I dare not hold you long today, but for a few minutes – allow me to share with you that God uses light throughout scripture. He led the children of Israel in the Old Testament by a pillar of fire out of their wilderness. David said in Psalm 119:105: Thy word is a lamp unto my feet, and a light unto my path.

Light is clearly important to God... so much so that God made light before the sun! Have you ever noticed that? So if there was no light source for the light to come from, the light must have been a release from Him... literally He made His own light! Not only that, but the main scripture I want you to consider today is John 1:1-5 – which says...

1:1 In the beginning was the Word, and the Word was with God, and the Word was God.

2 The same was in the beginning with God.

3 All things were made by him; and without him was not anything made that was made.

4 In him was life; and the life was the light of men.

5 And the light shineth in darkness; and the darkness comprehended it not.

As leaders, likely most of you have the responsibility of training and influencing the minds of people – in hopes of bettering or maybe enhancing the company or organization you are employed by. Why not lead like He does. By lighting the path!

A true leader not only provides knowledge but takes the initiative to lead the way in and with wisdom.

Okay with you all if I make an example to illustrate this? So everyone stand up please... thank you. Now, lights off please" All of the lights went off. It was dark in Salon D. "Now... even though you cannot see anything, your eyes are attempting to adjust to your new circumstances. Actually, all of your senses are attempting to recalibrate. Isn't it something how we will try to make up for our inabilities as leaders by utilizing our other strengths or by trying to overcome the negative circumstance by forcing our weakness to get stronger?"

You could tell by this point, even though it had been less than a minute, people were getting uncomfortable in the dark room. Small talk was beginning and people were beginning to reach around to try to seek comfort by knowing the room and persons in the room had not changed as far as they could tell.

"Bear with me, stay quiet please, ...thanks. Now, what I want you to do is try to find your way out of the room. There is more than one way out. Please try to find it."

As the nearly 100 persons stumbled around in the room, Debra began to search for her purse on the seat next to her. There it was – and in the side pocket was, yes, her flashlight... perfect. She turned it on – and within a moment, several people cheered and clapped. Without a word, Debra put the flashlight above her head and began to walk through the row of chairs, avoiding every blocked path to an exit door near the stage. As Les, Mickey and the remaining persons in the room followed Debra's every step, Debra said "we are almost out" and pushed the door to a very bright outdoor patio, where Pastor Chauncey stood – slowly clapping. As everyone exited the building, Pastor Chauncey began to speak again.

Thank you Miss. You led the entire group to a whole new environment. May I ask you, did you know where you were going?" Debra shook her head, nodding negatively.

"So, how did you know where to lead the group?"

Debra responded, "Well, I put the light above my head and followed the path that led me out of the darkness. I guess everyone else just followed me."

Pastor Chauncey smiled, "That is exactly right - you put the light above your head, above your own thoughts, your memories, your fears, your emotions and simply walked. Even though it appeared I was leading the group, you had the light. Even though others may have more experience in that old environment, you had the light. In spite of you being a female, you had the light – and you recognized nothing else mattered except following the light to the exit. Sometimes, you must lift your hands up in surrender, grab hold of your light and allow the light of God to lead you. If you let God lead you, more than your fears, more than your emotions, more than the ideas of the past, but allow Him to give you the wisdom to lead you and your groups out of dark situations, you will come out into a plush, green, joyous environment – outside of darkness.

I'm impressed that you did not try to go back the way that you came in; why was that?"

"To be honest, I basically forgot which direction I came from," Debra replied.

"Yes! It is easy to forget just how you got where you are when you are in darkness. I may have all of the knowledge from past experience, from the configuration in the room, even the people around me – but without illumination, well I am not able to see my way to anything."

You know, a lot of people would say 'I would like to be on my own doing my own thing, walking around – coming and going as I please but, if you don't have the light – well, you need to follow the one that has the light."

Debra abruptly asked "So, what is the light?"

"John 3 tells us that the light is Jesus and that the light came from God. I also want to share with you that God through His light gives you wisdom. You know, the Bible says 'if any man lacks wisdom let him ask of God who gives to all men liberally'. Only God gives wisdom... wisdom is from God and only by His Spirit can I really find what is needed at the moment to lead."

"So what is wisdom?" Mickey asks along with several others.

"Wisdom is the application of knowledge. I can't get wisdom from only my intelligence or even the totality of my experiences. There must be something else that grants me the ability to have what is needed to apply the knowledge in leadership.

Have you ever had a great idea and had no idea where it came from or even a team that brainstorms and the idea is brought to you as the leader and you implement it – even though it isn't your idea – and it ends up being a great success?" Several people nodded affirmatively. "That's because you had the God-given wisdom to implement an idea – no matter whose it was.

I have an example in the Bible. Many of you have heard the miracle where Jesus had two fish and five loaves of bread and fed over 5000 people with it, right? Well, remember, it was a child that brought the disciples the lunch. Jesus accepted the lunch and made it into what was needed and more. Without feeding the people, they would have possibly died right where they were. It was a miracle... because He, Jesus, had been enlightened and received the tools He needed from His team, even though He was the leader. Sometimes, you must know when to accept what someone else is offering you so that there can be provision for the next level for those that you lead. Leadership is not about your promotion, it's about your ability to bring people to their next and more prosperous destination.

You never know when you will need your light, ...in the work place, at a conference, you never know; but it is always good to have your *light* with you.

In the box on the patio table to my right, your left is a box full of flashlights that have the inscription 'You never know when you will need your light'. I trust that all of you have the light of God within you - with God, nothing is impossible. You have the wisdom to lead through the Light of God. His Light is above your knowledge (or lack of knowledge), fear, gender – anything. God will show you how to put your resources (your team, your education, your experience) all to good use. I submit to you today if you do not have a relationship with Jesus, for you to allow me to pray with you so that not only will you have salvation, but you will know the one who can lead you out of dark situations. Can I pray with you? May I?"

As several people began to walk forward, Debra with tears on her face just stood there. She thought about how she had tried everything to advance and it seemed like nothing worked. More education, more experience all amounted to more fear, more confusion. But she knew she needed to put God, the Light above her own fears and thoughts... she needed to, but could she really give her life to Jesus? As she stood there, emotionally torn, she looked back at her flashlight and read the inscription again. She remembered again how the light led her and many others behind her out of darkness.

She grabbed her light, turned it on, held it above her head and said, "Pastor Chauncey... I am ready to be led by the Light!" As she walked towards Pastor Chauncey, a few others did the same. Pastor Chauncey prayed for each of them, and dismissed service giving each of them a handful of extra lights to give to others.

Not much was said as Mickey, Les and Debra met at the doorway exiting to the beautiful morning again! Debra went on ahead walking the brief couple of blocks to the Sprint Center, to do some thinking. She also wanted to check in back at the company. She was trying resisting calling and focusing on this micro-managing thing, but she wasn't there yet. She had to know what was happening with the project launch and other stuff. Transformation and behavioral change don't just happen overnight you know.

Please use this page for notes.

...Day Two begins...

Breakout Session #5: Eliminate

Eliminate

- Bottlenecks / Conflicts
- Rumor Mindset
- Threatening Environments
- Bad Apple Acceptance
- Criticism as a Bad Thing

As the initial breakout session began Sunday morning, people were standing for the most part, talking about last night's events, some golf played, church this morning, day one learning's, the gorgeous morning all woke up to, etc. The facilitator Wendy, currently residing in Texas, flickered the room lights to get their attention. All pretty quickly found their seats, all in the same place as the day one sessions. Of course, you know how people are!

"Thanks, sorry for the light thing, but you guys are seemingly pretty wired; sounds like I missed a good talk last night over at the Power & Light District. I have some friends I was visiting with last night since I don't get to Kansas City very often.

Let me push on, we have lots to talk about and this breakout is one we always struggle getting through all the material."

Several minutes were spent reflecting on some of yesterdays learning, and a few questions asked in clarification. It was obvious the content of the Great 8 Principles was causing some good thinking and learning.

"First of all, some of you, as you think of the topic of this session, have thought about the TQM, or quality concept of eliminating waste? You probably noticed, right? Well don't think we didn't think of that, because we did", she said grinning.

"There are reasons it's not on the list, even though it could be obviously. Let me share our thinking on this. We absolutely believe that all of these up there could and would eliminate waste in your most important and valuable resource or system …your people system! We just didn't want this to get looking like an Operations Quality program, even though well it absolutely *is* in so many ways. It is likely the best *quality* program you or your company could ever take on; fixing leaders and leadership. The quality of the leader is about the quality of the organization. We believe and know that when the leader changes, then the organization, or team changes. Think on that for a moment." Wendy, the facilitator walked to the other side of the room and turned to speak, but was interrupted.

"First of all, yes, you *should* have been there last night. In fact a piece of your topic here about bad apples was talked about." coming from Robin, a senior manager and Performance Systems Leader.

In briefly introducing herself, since she had said little to this point; all learned she lived on the Missouri side of Kansas City and worked on the Kansas side of Kansas City. There were those in attendance who indicated they never realized Kansas City included both Kansas and Missouri. All agreed that a lesson in Geography might be in order, but in fact we should get back to this leadership thing! She then went on to make some pretty astute observations about the bad apple concept; she also shared her faith story, witnessing a bit as Booker had told them all to do as leaders.

Wendy, after taking some comments regarding the lessons learned about the bad apple concept, seemed convinced that that topic had been well covered. For the benefit of three who missed, a brief review took place. She then asked about conflict and its fit into leadership.

Chuck, one of a couple of IT guys among the group from North Kansas City, responded when the facilitator looked at him for input. "Well this might surprise some folks, what with me being an IT guy, but I actually am pretty schooled on the whole conflict thing. I realized maybe five or six years back that I had to get smart on facilitating conflict resolution. Could I just share some of my thinking for a minute or two?" As Chuck looked around being urged to go on, he stood and walked toward the front and side of the room to see all.

"First of all as we would likely all agree with, people will be in conflict, accept it, that is a fact. To have conflict, we only need people working together, then we have all the necessary ingredients," Chuck looked inquiringly as he received plenty of agreement.

"The issue may be anything, from implementing a new management program to exactly where we should place the wastebasket! Maybe the most significant takeaway I could share with you is this one which I share frequently. Just because people oppose your thought, idea or way of doing something, doesn't make them an enemy! This seems obvious, but trust me, we all have a tendency to go there when we face another's perspective or opposing point of view. This goes back and for sure reinforces what we spoke to in our Relate session yesterday. Build relationships quickly before something happens, because it will.

People have to work with people that they or we did not, and maybe would not have likely chosen, if it had been our choice. Unlike other situations, like church, school and/or some other social setting where we get to choose those that we want to be with, at work it is rarely our decision. In those other situations, we can walk away at any time; it is not the same in the work environment. Therefore, you must get along with others or face conflict....or leave, which rarely seems to be a good option."

Chuck was smiliing and ready to begin another thought when Kenisha piped up, "Chuck if I may, I would like to toss in something here. Something I came across a while back, posed the following ideas about organizational conflict. Conflict between people can probably be broken down into one of two categories, personality or job-related. Although we all tend to jump to the conclusion that any opposition means there is a personality conflict present; this source said that is normally not the case.

More often than not, it is more a matter of something within the job structure that is placing people into conflict. A few of possibilities might be people with different expectations, folks sharing of resources like computers, forklifts, space, or any number of things; unclear reporting structures like those dotted line situations; miscommunication itself, overlapping roles or job functions, differences in standards; pay inequality, and so on.

Picture two co-workers having to share one computer. Management and the organization's budget figures that one computer ought to be enough; assuming that the people will share appropriately and fairly. You and I know that this is not always the case; adults don't often play much better than kids do we?"

Someone in back threw into the discussion, "Another dynamic that does seem to be prevalent and cause significant conflict in our company is what I call the 'only one answer mentality'. Many individuals, departments and the organization overall seem to possess this thinking and mindblock to some degree. People tend to think, 'You are right as long as you agree with me' ...or ...'I'm right, therefore you must be wrong.' As our facilitator pointed out, the enemy factor often times is in play."

Wendy responded, "This is all really good, that was awesome guys, thanks. Let me share some of the stuff we would add to all you have already hit on, some logic we discovered that managers often possess. Leaders tend at times, to not deal with conflict for some of the following reasons, things like its personal, not my business, they will work it out; no tools to facilitate resolution; dislike of confrontation; a fear of taking sides or judging one over the other; I will just make it worse, or the ultimate, ...I don't have time to mess with it!

What we believe here and are saying to you the leader is this, the reality is that we must deal with conflict. It is a leader's job! It is *always* your business! Why?... because people in conflict, to some degree are affecting productivity, teamwork, communication, relationships, morale, ...need I say more?

There are many models out there to deal with conflict resolution. Let me just offer here a couple of concepts that need to be part of whatever model you utilize:

> • Force them to listen to each other
> ...yes, you can force listening!
>
> • Buy-in must occur
> ...it cannot be YOUR solution, it must be
> THEIRS!
>
> • Accountability must be the last step
> ...we all come back together to review
> status
>
> "If these don't happen, it didn't
> happen!"

We have placed a copy of a specific model in your materials. If there are any questions before you leave or after you get back home, just holler at us."

Debra in a low quiet tone, shared as he finished, "Take the time now or you *will* spend much more later; it's that *pay me now or pay me later* thing? Boy have I messed this up in my past."

Plenty of agreement was shared along with a few stories. The stories were cut off, "Forgive me but let's press on with a couple of the other bullets", the facilitator said as she gestured toward the overview on the wall. "How about bottlenecks, you guys heard of this concept?"

A few folks ventured some thinking, as Wendy jumped back in, "Going back to my initial comments regarding qualilty, waste, and so forth. Let me share this with you. A year or so after one of these conferences, one of the facilitators, the lady you will meet in your next breakout session, came up with this. She said she was processing a discussion on topics like conflict, relationships, etc when it struck her that people systems, teams and operational systems collectively deal with and have bottlenecks in common. You that are here from the manufacturing world, or anyone who has dealt with Lean Manufacturing, TQM, Six Sigma, and so on will definitely recognize the dynamic of bottlenecks. So we're on common ground. Let me offer this definition for bottleneck. It is a point within a process/system where the flow and/or productivity is slowed down and where extra effort or resources must be expended to address the problem. You won't find that in Webster's, just something we worked up here among us.

Now, here's what might be a new perspective on some old concepts regarding teamwork. Consider this for a moment—teams function much like any operation or process, ...your people-system. It is a matter of everything being in sync, but instead of machinery and equipment, we are speaking of working relationships, roles and expectations understood, and so on. Each operation or person must support others for teamwork to flow. When people function well together, the result is a highly efficient, synergetic, and productive process.

That is precisely what team-building is all about, isn't it? The challenge of improving and eliminating bottlenecks. As with conflicts, teams have bottlenecks. It is not productive to be sitting there thinking of Bob, Sue, or someone else that you view as a current relationship problem. We don't eliminate by laying blame on players individually. In reality we do or we might, but we shouldn't. It is about eliminating the wasteful bottleneck.

We all become bottlenecks in our team people-systems at times, and these have an impact on the overall success of the people systems. We effect the pace, productivity, quality, synergy, etc, ...of the team. Here are some of the bottlenecks that we have come up with, that definitely bottle things up to some degree for some amount of time, until identified and resolved, or eliminated. In your packets, you will find a handout called bottlenecks; grab it and I am going to let you think on them for a moment. I'll also put it up on the screen:

Bottlenecks in People Systems

• **PAST ISSUES** (problems that individuals have had with others on the team that have not been addressed…but, rather, carried around as baggage or grudges or, minimally, uncooperativeness)
• **ATTITUDES / NEGATIVISM** (some of us don't realize how important these overused words are…when I outwardly express my negative attitude, others see and avoid it)
• **COMMUNICATION** (when I fail to communicate openly and effectively with other team members, it affects the overall efficiency of the team)
• **UNCLEAR ROLES / EXPECTATIONS** (can be a failure of the organization or leaders to clarify functional areas OR that a team member sees their role one differently than everyone else)
• **CONFLICTS / MISUNDERSTANDINGS** (someone did or said something that you took the wrong way…personalities, job-related, diversity, culture, etc.)
• **RELATIONS / TRUST** (openness, honesty, understanding, and acceptance of others…trust in each other to do their part, fulfill commitments, meet deadlines; respect feelings, opinions, and thoughts)
• **CAPABILITY** (knowledge, know-how, education, training, and experience to do the job; skill level)
• **NEW PLAYERS** (people new to the team can't become productive until trust and relationships are established

So. the message to leaders is to understand and realize the impact of bottlenecks on the team's productivity and ultimate success. It's not just what you should deal with… again, it's your job. As leaders we need to train and grow our team and team-members to take responsibility to help other members of the team, their peers to overcome their bottlenecks. Leaders need to learn to identify them and then take action. The sooner we deal with them, the sooner we become a well-oiled machine, operation, system, and team!"

Jack, from the back, tossed in at this point, "I will just add this, last but not least, when we do nothing about these situations, but just allow them to exist day after day after day, then we are practicing 'insanity. We all know that definition, 'doing the same thing over and over and over again, and then expecting different results.' That's what unresolved conflict, and for that matter unresolved bottlenecks, looks like. FYI, I have been there, done, that, and still possess the tee-shirt!"

Everyone chuckled and made comments from personal experiences, as Robin again chimed in, "I heard on some TV show a while back, it was about the workplace and management; it spoke to your bullet up there on gossiping, etc. Well I think it does anyway?"

Everyone urged her to go ahead and share, "Well we all know and have allowed it, done it and it goes on all the time, rumors and gossip. The talk show host was saying enormous strides can be made toward increased teamwork, trust, less conflict, more productivity and improved relationships all the way around, when and if we can control it.

It is *not* just part of human nature and inevitably going to be there, unless we, the leader allow it. The host was sharing that he sees this within groups and has been caught up in it himself. He went on to explain how we do this to each other and the damage that it inflicts.

A scenario he used went like, say you have a problem with someone. It is something about something they said, what you thought they said, their opinion, something they did that impacted your world, etc...get the picture? What do we typically do when this occurs? We go share and bellyache about it with someone else, a peer, a boss, anyone and everyone except the person who really needs to hear it!

It was kind of humorously shared but really made you think. Teammates will even take it straight to the leader to deal with. Think of the impact and fallout of doing things this way; first of all the person you are taking it to can do nothing but listen to your bellyaching, right? What are we expecting them to do with it? If they go do something with it, then they have broken your trust!?! If you allow them or urge them to do it for you, all you are going to do is lose respect and your relationship with that individual. Round and round it all goes.

Teams that are ready to fix this dynamic have to honestly sit down, look each other in the eye and say 'we all have our gripes with each other for good reason, but why don't we agree to start doing things in the right way in the right spirit...?' After all, if you tell me what your issue is or what you don't like that I did or whatever, haven't you actually done something positive regarding our relationship and the team overall? But we tend to take confrontation and disagreement as world-shattering stuff instead of the good that is to be gained if resolved. If we can manage to do it in a respectful, tactful and non-confrontational way...it can drastically improve a team in ways we cannot even imagine.

Rumors, gossip, and telling the wrong person, this stuff tears down relationships, discourages communication, kills trust and makes life miserable for all around the issue. Not to mention all the wasted time, there's that waste thing again guys," she paused momentarily, "I hope that made some sense, I'm sure you get it anyway".

After listening to a few acknowledgements and follow up thoughts regarding what Robin had said, the facilitator concluded, "I guess you pretty well hit this gossip and rumors thing. As leaders, mentors and even as team members, we can help others by steering them to the right person, maybe after a moment of empathetic listening of course. We must not forget to be coaching and teaching them why we are sending them away. We need to be teaching our people all of this stuff, what Robin just shared, etc and address this wrong kind of behavior.

"Now," as Wendy broke into sharing a grin, "do some thinking on all this and be ready when you go to fixing all this. Think what you have told them to do, the position you will be putting them in, when *you* come talking about someone?"

Everyone broke out in laughter and also acknowledged it was a good point. There was some obvious sarcasm about how no leader would ever do such a thing.

"I would also just add about rumors that we as leaders can help with it by not keeping secrets. Share stuff early and frequently, because when we try to keep something a secret, no matter what it is, we will pay for it. The rumor mill will go to work." This coming from the lady next to Debra, who again impressed the group with her insight, "CEO's, presidents and senior execs fester and cause this when they are working on high powered decisions and agree among each other to keep it under their hats until it is all figured out. It goes back to that change discussion we had in the other breakout session, right? When we go that route, the word always gets out. I tell you this from some pretty painful experiences learning this deal."

Wendy raising her hands to get the attention of all, "Thanks, that's a great point and so real, too. We do have to end this session, but I do want to share with you about 'Teamership.' No one really knows where the term came from, and if someone else deserves the credit, we are happy for them to have it. But regardless, this is a message about you, each of us as leaders working with other leaders. Let me share in our brief last minutes here, it's again never really become a definition but just a dynamic for us all to be aware of, working with peers, other leaders.

Many of us here have been involved in training, facilitating, coaching and consulting in the areas of individual and organizational leadership for a number of years now. Personally I have begun to realize and understand more and more about this dynamic and phenomenon over the last few years or so. So what is this teamership thing, you ask?...thanks for asking. We have all dealt with many supervisors and managers with various skill-levels of leadership effectiveness. Some who have much still to learn...some who possess a great understanding of leadership....some who I have learned much from...some who think they understand and practice it well, but really don't. Everybody here falls into one of these categories to some degree.

What we hear and see in nonverbal tones, from many leaders is 'I already know that leadership stuff...' We here know some of you skeptics in the room right here came here thinking some of this stuff, ...didn't you now?

So what is Teamership?...again, thanks for asking, I'm getting there really. Many managers in fact, do know leadership and may even be practicing and working on it continually downward, with those they lead. What they are not practicing so well however is teamership.

Here is just a possible definition - Teamership is the act of leaders practicing teamwork as a team-member, on their own team, while not being the leader of the team. It is the functioning as a peer and/or follower as part of a management group reporting to a higher authority, his/her leader, maybe your CEO or president!

To give you an example, take a senior VP management staff or even a group of mid-level managers; who all have their own leadership and management roles and functions. You would logically expect them to work together as a team, right?

It's ironic that often times leaders exhibit behaviors while in the peer or followership role that would be unsatisfactory if one of their own people did the same stuff! Think about it...when my perspective changes and I'm no longer the leader but now I'm just one of the team; it becomes a completely different challenge for us. I guess it is just that they have forgotten how to or never really focused or learned how to function unless he or she is in charge.

This is kind of an amazing concept to me, ...why can't leaders practice that 'stuff' that they expect of their own followers and practice it themselves?

Teamwork is a much used word that takes on a new meaning when an experienced, seasoned manager must work with other seasoned leaders to achieve someone else's goals and expectations.   Maybe it's the subconscious saying "I've already done this follower thing and I want to be in charge, ...I don't know, it's kind of weird, but very real.

I am guessing some of you are resembling these remarks, aren't you now?"

Kendra popped into the conversation, "Leading leaders is another level of leadership development that many top executives and managers are challenged and struggle with as they climb the ladder of success."

Wendy was quick to add, "We have some programs and deliverables that we could help your organization with on this," she said winking at the group and smiling.

Lauren interrupted, "I suspect that we can never really know that leadership stuff as you put it. Likely when and if you ever think you do, you better get ready to be surprised. I have to tell you, before I got here, maybe just within the week prior, I think I used those very words with my own boss, ...yikes."

Everyone looked at her empathetically and then reflectively broke out in smiles; someone hollered from the back, "Ain't learning a great thing!"

Someone else followed up quickly, "You got it, and I'll add here, I strongly believe in *never stop learning*. Boy has that concept been beaten into me and maybe all of us over the last couple of days, what say gang?"

Wendy cut off any more conversation, "Thanks, you guys were great. We do have to wrap up; before we do, let's do that Connections thing now with five principles under your belt. Betting you will all pretty much really be seeing how cool these principles reinforce and support each other. Each most definitely does play a key part in the other seven principles. Let's see what your thoughts are. Here pass these around please."

Eliminate: Great 8 Connections & 'food for thought'…

Notice how the other seven concepts support, reinforce, and connect with this one.

FACILITATE …discussion and understanding of the importance of identifying waste.

ACCOMMODATE …receptiveness of seeing, hearing, and considering elimination.

DEMONSTRATE …model; be proactive in identifying unproductiveness.

COMMUNICATE …relate and inform identified waste, barriers, and ineffectiveness.

RELATE …nonproductive relations resulting in nonproductive communication.

EVALUATE …continual improvement; always assess productivity, adding value.

CREATE …new approaches, assessments, and ways of identification.

Please make your own notes and comments below.

"No doubt your connecting the dots now regarding the principles; thanks for a great discussion on the Connections info. I really appreciate your honesty here and urge you to remember that *awareness* is a first huge step to ever learning anything. See you guys at this afternoon's final wrap-up session. Catch me here later on or holler at me any time after you return home. We have a great brunch out there now before your next session, don't miss it. Take care and God bless."

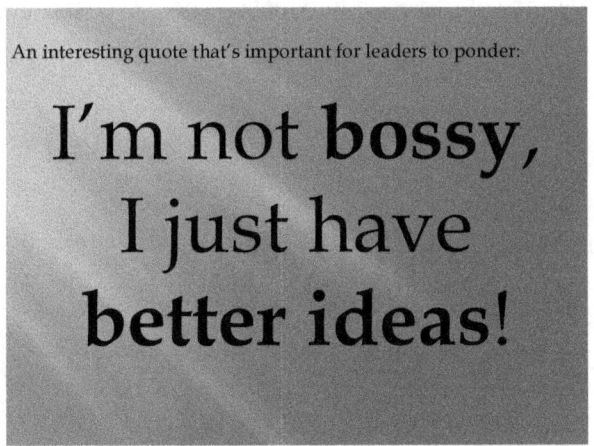

An interesting quote that's important for leaders to ponder:

I'm not **bossy**, I just have **better ideas!**

Debra chuckled to herself, considering the concepts she just heard, as she was heading to the next session. Conflict among people was indeed inevitable; she also knew that her team had an extraordinary amount of conflict. There was also a fair amount between herself and peers at the company; that had to be fixed she determined.

She knew that these professional conflicts cost time, production delays, rework, money and yes, waste. She decided to capture her notes regarding the conflict model here as well.

Debra also thought that if she had her team issues addressed and working towards a collaborative environment that while conflict would still occur, it would be healthy conflict and debate that the people who were actually doing the work had a say in the "how" details of the work being completed. She knew that there were some strong personalities she would need to coach through the process to make sure "we" had strong and supportable action items.

She quickly calculated her production delay costs and all of the downstream impacts:

Debra's Notes about ROI after Breakout #5

Inventory Costs + Overtime Costs + Contract Penalties...

Our largest orders this year incurred penalties because the company didn't deliver on time. While it wasn't anyone's fault in particular, the root of the problem was lack of cooperation driven by unhealthy conflict.

Ponder this thing they call "teamership" and my opinion of the HR manager, the warehouse supervisor, and others I work with...

<u>Reasons Leaders Don't Get Involved in Conflict Resolution</u>

- Don't like confrontation
- Fear of taking sides
- No time to mess with it
- No tools (like this model)
- Might take care of itself
- I might make it worse!?

<u>I Like This Model Because…</u>

- It is time efficient
- It prevents the leader from judging / taking sides
- They solve their own problem
- It forces listening to happen
- It provides a tool for the leader.

<u>Facilitator Follows These Steps</u>

1) Bob states the problem as Bob sees it…
2) Sally repeats what Bob has said—not agrees, but repeats
3) Bob concurs that Sally understands his thoughts—or doesn't
…If not, Bob restates the problem as he sees it, then Sally repeats, then Bob concurs, and so on.
4-6) Repeat 1-3 with Sally stating the problem…

<u>The Biggest Problem I've Identified in myself is forced listening—HUGE deal, and I'm not proficient</u>

7) Discussion, search for alternatives / options.
8) Agreement on something that worked out / solution. For example: Bob takes computer in the morning, Sally in the afternoon.
9) Accountability Step: Agreement to everyone to return soon, over the next few days, and discuss how the agreement is working. If it isn't working, start over.
10) Go try it!

What are the outcomes? It's never fun, but it's time efficient. Leader never gave input, just facilitated. The team solves their problem, not me. It's about them. Buy in, ownership, consensus stuff—resembles the basic problem solving model!

[What about ROI? Conflicts resolved! Very valuable, indeed!]

Please use this page for notes.

Kid and Dog Update ...Brunch & Headaches

Mickey was outside the door of Les's breakout session, just as he arrived. "I just got a call from Jackson. He's pretty down; it seems the coach brought in Jackson and a couple of others who are at risk of not being able to compete at the state meet. He lectured them on the importance of education, accountability, and stuff like that. Anyway, Jackson said it was really a pretty motivating talk, but in the end, nothing was resolved. The coach just left it hanging, Jackson still doesn't know about his status for the meet."

"He didn't tell him anything?" Les was frustrated, and upset although he knew this was not something at this point for him to interfere with. The parent in him thought it better to leave it to the leader there, his coach; changing topics, he asked, "How about the dog?"

"Well I wish I was here with some good news, but that's nothing good either. Jackson said Doc believes Chief isn't going to make it. Not a done deal yet, but it just isn't looking good. He seems to just still be very subdued, hurting and well, still in a state of shock. I wish you weren't in this conference; I don't want to be alone right now. I guess I love that dog more than I realized."

Les offered to skip the next session, but Mickey insisted he not do that. She would be OK and would find them over the lunch break. She indicated some words from the sermon they heard this morning were actually pretty fitting here and were helping her cope. They both agreed there was no reason to go share any of this with Debra just now.

During the brunch break, Dr. Scott Chorny, a close friend and chiropractor of Booker's, was introduced and provided an informative talk about the Headache Relief Center. He made many interesting points about stress and while the three massage therapists he brought with him worked on folks, he spoke of the impact of headaches, stress and health on productivity in the workplace.

More than a couple of people came up after his talk, sharing stories of lifelong headache pain issues and how exciting this was to hear. Many spoke of friends, their employees and family members with life-altering pain. He ran out of cards quickly and was sharing his website instead.

One lady spoke with the doctor one on one sharing an amazing personal story of health issues, to include migraines. She was trying to figure out how to stay over until Monday to get to Dr. Scott's office in Olathe, KS (south KC area).

Breakout Session #6: Facilitate

Facilitate

- Consensus in ALL
- Continued Improvement
- Your PEOPLE System
- Teaching Fishing
- Grow Individual and TEAM
- 100% versus Anything Less

"This is probably the favorite session for all of us facilitators," Ana, the facilitator was off and rolling before the last person was even seated.

Before getting into the discussion, Ana shared her background of Puerto Rico, the military, now in nursing, a heroic situation she had been involved with a few years back and recently completing her MBA. An impressive lady and professional; she was amazing. Ana had connected with Booker through her MBA studies and was now working to help him translate books and materials into Spanish.

"The reason is because it just touches all the others so closely. What we are after here is just to truly get the essence of facilitation in our minds and souls, and to begin eliminating, see there's that *Eliminate* concept, ...the mindset created during our whole lives practically. Lecturing, dictating, directing, teaching, managing, coaching, etc all take on new meaning when we can translate them and maybe even transform them into thinking clearly and easily."

"I get it, I think." Debra had chimed in first, "but what I want to get is a fair amount of thinking on the ROI of this. I'm not against it and believe I practice it, at least to some extent. I just think that it is also our job to direct, teach, make decisions and maybe even lecture at times. So again, I'm just looking for the payoff, the payoff of taking all the time that facilitating takes, when I can direct and tell someone the answer immediately and be onto other stuff."

There was a lot of muttering, side conversations and discussion that began immediately, from both perspectives. The teaching fishing concept spoken to in an earlier session was raised again. Lots of points were made of the value of asking what people think, facilitating the improvement of their knowledge, thinking, and self-confidence among other benefits. Just then, Ana broke in tossing a book to Debra.

"Here, that is Booker's first book, the one on Teaching Fishing. It is yours, do yourself a favor and read it. I think it will resolve all this completely for you. We always give away a couple just because...there are always a couple of Debra's, I mean skeptics here," all started smiling and laughing gesturing at her. "Just messing with you; truly that's not a bad on you my friend. This really and truly is a huge change of mindset for any leader. Going from what we have watched our whole lives and suddenly when we are in charge, doing it differently from the model. Please sincerely go through it, it's a very easy read, but lots of good stuff there, trust me."

Jack spoke up as Ana concluded the thought, "If I may, I am trying to do what you were saying there Ana; trying to process this, internalize it and well get my arms around this facilitation thing. Facilitate or to lead...facilitating, leading.... facilitator, leader—these two words and concepts are remarkably similar. Facilitating seems to be more about the teaching or learning process while leading is commonly about the directing, managing, and motivating of people in the work process.

I went to a university workshop a year or so ago. I teach with a couple of schools and the one was really making a major push toward transforming our teachers from being lecturers and becoming more, yes facilitators. It was pretty eye opening and here's where I am with it. This was all hugely interesting to me, not just as a faculty member part time but also being a manager in my company.

When we take a hard look at the action aspect of each, they actually merge amazingly." Jack spoke to the topic for a good couple of minutes making some great points.

The woman next to Debra spoke up as he paused to provide an opportunity for someone else to talk, "I also do some academic teaching. Facilitating is most often associated with learning in the academic arena as an technique of teaching to consider. In facilitation, we do not force or make the learner learn; rather it is about facilitating the process of learning or causing learning to happen by using various techniques. These may include, but are not limited to: encouraging discussion, learner doing activities, using the learner's ideas and experiences, having the learner teach, practicing a skill, etc. We frequently hear other terms used in the learning world such as teaching, training, lecturing, speaking, etc. Now in applying this to leading, I'm kind of like Debra here, and still working on it a bit myself."

Ana decided to take the lead back, "This is good, you guys are thinking. Let me toss in a couple of points and maybe it will pick up precisely where you guys just left it. Leading is most often associated with getting people to accomplish tasks through some methods or techniques or skills. To effectively lead people, a leader uses such things as encouraging involvement, soliciting ideas, team problem-solving, listening,etc. The word leader itself is often replaced with words such as supervisor, manager, president, director, coordinator, CEO, etc. Interestingly there are similarities as well on the negative side of these two terms as well. The true facilitator of learning will not attempt to make someone learn by cramming information into them, forcing them to memorize, testing to ensure they know it, lecturing, telling them that this and that are important, etc. For us here, the true leader realizes that one cannot truly lead by telling, directing, forcing, threatening, making all decisions, not asking for input, and so on. That's just managing and maintaining the way things are now and have always been.

Facilitating and leading are both about selling the need for and causing involvement and buy-in into the process to cause real learning to occur or accomplish goals and objectives. Either of these roles in a very pure sense could be called either one of these names, leader or facilitator. They could be interchangeable, sure. They are both about the leading and facilitating of a process. To effectively lead or facilitate, there are common skills required. The art or skill of motivating others, involving others in the process, developing the thinking skills of others, coaching, listening, respecting and sincerely wanting their ideas, creating a non-threatening environment, coaching and recognizing other's performance and the list goes on and on!

Whether we are speaking of the classroom, the office, on the factory floor or on a sports team, …if we are doing it well, we are facilitating and leading. In the classroom at any level, the one teaching is the leader and the students are the team."

Robin butted in, chuckling, "Ana you got me thinking, from that movie, uh, mmmm, Field of Dreams, that phrase in it, 'build it and he will come'. It seems that on the flip side, in the workworld, the supervisor or manager is the facilitator; he or she is facilitating the process of accomplishing whatever it is to be done. As the manager in the work-situation, we need to be able to see and understand that we are the teacher and the employees or subordinates are the students. If they are not learning, growing or improving , then leading and or facilitating isn't happening! The picture is clear as I think about it - the crusty ol' office manager or shop supervisor who just shouts orders, as well as the old-timer senior manager or professor just continually preaching and directing the same thing day in and day out. Nobody is progressing or learning really, but they just continue to try to force it, make them, dictate, tell them, micro manage, discipline them, etc, etc, etc. I'm almost done here, but I am now tieing this back to the Evaluate session, we are facilitating that continual improvement, monthly performance improvement process. We can't make them be better, but we can facilitate a process that will result in their improvement. I have to stop and write some things down here; someone else go for it."

"Robin, you are so right. We are back again to that old definition of insanity, 'doing the same thing over and over and over again, following the leader, and expecting different results." Ana had cut in picking up the lead in the dialogue, "Now one might say *so what* to this whole line of thought and reasoning; suggesting that it's just semantics and words. No argument from us here for sure. Likely it doesn't really matter what word we use to describe any of these roles. What matters is, are the people in either case truly learning, growing, developing or are they just passing tests or doing what they're told and picking up a paycheck?!? The real question is, are you leading and/or facilitating, ...or are you managing, dictating, developing little and lecturing?

The dynamic of change does play in big time when we think of facilitation and that only makes sense. But try to wrap your minds around this, addressed a bit earlier, probably yesterday. If you are leading, *everything* you are doing is about change. Not some but just possibly everything. If we are leading vs managing, you see, we are not maintaining. Without a big discussion here on managing vs leading, we here just believe and preach that leaders grow, while managers maintain. Sure leaders also need some management skills, but primarily if they are really leading, they are continually improving everything by facilitating. Facilitating people growing, systems improving, the team getting better, the relationships developing, bottlenecks eliminated, creating, accomodating, demonstrating, and so forth.

See, there we are again, all these eight concepts are just so hugely inter-twined and reinforce and compliment each other. Thus the development of the great eight concepts to develop the great eight leader!"

"Debra, hope you are getting all this ROI stuff, because that is what we have been talking to I think," coming from her buddy tossing in those two cents. "I want to briefly chime in here and just say that to the bullet up there, synergy, that again is what and why we need to be facilitating. If we maintain the team as it is, there may be a bit of synergy for most teams. However, from my experience, there really isn't much. If I am facilitating the team and individuals growing in their communications, relating, eliminating, and so on. I am developing or facilitating better and better synergy. Am I making sense?"

All absolutely concurred and Ana just let things sit quiet for a moment or two. She slowly wandered around the right side toward the back of the room. She then offered, "Debra, what are you seeing, thinking...?"

Debra fidgeted a bit, turning toward Ana and most of the room, then saying, "Well, to tell you the truth I am still digesting it, but what I was jotting down here to think about later was just how facilitation ties to all the great eight concepts. I am looking at the list, communicate, relate, evaluate, create, accommodate, etc. I facilitate all of these, I facilitate improved communications, or I don't. I do or don't facilitate improving relationships, the process of feedback and performance evaluation, decision making, creating new ways, and so on. Not sure what any of that means, but as I talk out loud here, I am just thinking that if I am doing those things, there has to be huge ROI, huge improved productivity, bottom line profits, oh my gosh. I see why this is never really effectively presented or understood, this ROI thing. It is a bit challenging to put numbers to it, but I have to think right now, that all this leadership stuff would just have to pay off."

Ana was back up front as Debra finished, "I am just thinking I don't think I am going to facilitate one more thing here. That seems to be a great way to let this session end. However I don't want to stymie any questions or other thoughts; anyone have anything else?"

Someone from the back mumbled something about the importance of relationship to this facilitation concept. It was discussed a bit as the group essentially reached consensus on how relationship, communication, trust and some other things had to be in place for good synergy to get facilitated.

"Hey it's connections time, right?" Debra had butted in as things were coming to an obvious conclusion.

Ana agreed and handed out the sheets for Debra to pass out.

Facilitate: Great 8 Connections & 'food for thought'…

Notice how the other seven concepts support, reinforce, and connect with this one.

ACCOMMODATE …internal and external customer receptiveness, service and input.

DEMONSTRATE …professional, open, and respectful attitude in meetings and other interpersonal interactions.

COMMUNICATE …clearly; involving all, not just some exchanges of information and ideas.

RELATE …maintenance of relations in all directions; development of new relations.

EVALUATE …instrumental in decision-making and problem solving processes.

CREATE …creativity facilitates improvement; facilitation improves creativity

ELIMINATE …distrust, negativity—threats to effectiveness, leading teams, and meetings.

Please make your own notes and comments below.

Debra immediately tossed in some revelations she had had during the first two sessions today; she even seemed to get a bit emotional. It seemed her skepticism was slowly, or maybe quickly, eroding.

Facilitation in respect to decision making and consensus received more than a few minutes of discussion before they stopped, were dismissed and headed out the door. Ana clicked the remote displaying the last slide, shaking hands and getting a couple of hugs as well. Debra gave her one, a big one, as Ana handed her a box of tissues.

Leader's Purpose

We are not here as the best ones to make decisions; we are here to get the best decisions made.

The best decisions come from the hearts and minds of everyone involved.

We are here to facilitate that most valuable of resources: our People System!

Debra's Notes about ROI after Breakout #6

...I plan to engage and start building. The WE in TEAM includes everyone involved in the decision-making process. I've acted as if the majority ruled, asking for my team's input and opinions, but really never... I was always actually just trying to appease them making them feel, well, STUPID!

I will set some ground rules, moderate and reserve the ultimate decision-making—I am committed to have THEM, the team, discuss, collaborate, debate, and cooperate in the final decision. BUY IN!

It won't be easy, however, the data and potential ROI outweighs my own personal interests (and desire to solve things, make decisions)....so I AM committed to making this work.

Developing my staff?! They probably aren't ready for the workshop I'm in right now, however, I do think that individual development would help to make the team better and would feed into the overall improved performance.

I probably spend about 45% of my time on administrative tasks, meetings, and other non-managerial duties, plus traveling, the kind of training I'm doing now, taking breaks, special projects, customer service stuff, etc.

I may only spend 30% of my time actually managing, leading, and coaching my people!

I need to do some research on development and teams. One woman in the group mentioned that she had found some great information and ideas on a Web site after doing some research. I think she mentioned "Mckinsey Quarterly dot com." I'll check it out.

Please use this page for notes.

Debra Catches Up with Booker

"Booker?" Debra called. In between breakout sessions, Debra was close to shouting across the foyer. He was with another gentleman and both stopped and looked backward; as Debra caught up with them. "Can I abuse your time for a minute and share something?"

"Sure, but let me quickly introduce you to Tim Goodwin first. Tim is a good friend, a leader in many respects and is in Financial Services. We invite him along to talk to attendees if they wish any financial assistance, advice, help and all. Tim handed her a card, shook hands as he glanced back at Booker, "Great meeting you ... Booker I'll let you guys talk. I'll see you at the After Action Review later on this afternoon."

As they finished their conversation, Debra flipped the card over and saw a handwritten note:

A favorite quote of mine
"Do not go to where the path may lead. Instead go to where there is no path, and leave a trail"
-Ralph Waldo Emerson

Financial Services!

- Life Insurance
- Investments
- Debt Solutions
- Identity Protection
- & More!

Tim Goodwin
508.499.9324
tgoodwin@primerica.com

Booker gestured for Debra to come over and sit down in a couple of large straight back easy chairs in the corner, "What's up, and forgive me, but your name is?"

"Thanks," Debra responded sitting in the other chair, "I'm Debra from TBI, in Seattle. I'm here with my boss and his wife as well. Great meeting you, how are things going here with the conference?"

He broke into a grin and immediately responded, "You tell me. How *are* we doing?"

Debra leaned forward in her chair, twisting more directly facing him, "Well this is a perfect lead in, thanks for asking. That's precisely why I asked to speak with you. I wanted to just tell you, well, I was one of those skeptics. Maybe the biggest negative attitude that was here when you opened up things here yesterday."

Booker inquired, "Okay...and now?"

"Well I have to tell you, honestly this has been tremendous. I was not here to be won over easily, but I must say, you have; and we're not even quite finished. I am getting the ROI aspect and that's what I came for; don't tell my boss just yet, but I am buying in!" Debra leaned back smiling, and returned to the front edge of her chair focusing on Booker.

Leaning back, crossing his legs and grinning even more than she was, "Well come on, feed me, what went wrong with your plan?" Booker said chuckling.

"Well I am still processing all that. I have to get to that next breakout, so I can't go into it all here just now. Let's just say, I am close to becoming a believer. And that's not about your talk last night, which by the way was awesome, and I am a Believer in that sense. But a believer now also in what I used to call this warm and fuzzy leadership stuff. I believe I have come to know the real meaning of my boss's favorite quote and one you guys have used here as well. That one you know 'people don't care how much you know....'"

"...until first they know how much you care," he had cut her off completing the second part of the quote. "That relationship dynamic is huge isn't it? We here are always amazed at how many managers and organizations just don't get the true power of relationships and well for sure, leadership. Glad it has impacted you. You figure you will actually lead differently now? You're not just caught up in the emotion of all this warm and fuzzy stuff ...are you now?"

"No, it's not that for sure. There is so much I have taken away here already. I am absolutely going to involve those all around me, 360 degrees around me as was mentioned here. I'm going to ask them to hold me accountable to being different, to become a more effective leader. I'm afraid it will take a bit of eating crow; a bit of mending some fences; apologizing to some even. That won't be much fun, but that's okay, I can do it.

This is kind of personal but if I may ...I was divorced less than a year ago, and I think until these last couple of days here, I did not realize how much it had impacted me. All this is about getting close relationships established. To tell the truth, after being abandoned by my husband, I was pretty bruised up. What has hit me here is that because of that happening to me, without going into all too much, I have been keeping my distance in relationships. My trust in maybe even mankind was wounded; and it has been really hurting my management, my leadership, I am seeing that so clear now."

"Debra, that's an amazing realization you have made. I am guessing *that* awareness is going to actually help you heal and begin growing and becoming happier and better in both worlds—your management and your personal life!" Booker was now leaning forward and reached out to grasp her hand.

She grasped his hand being offered, and stood up slowly, "Booker, thanks so much here, thanks for taking a few moments. I had no idea I was going to share all that, and hope I didn't take advantage of you or make you feel uncomfortable. I better get now before I miss something, and I know now I need all of this I can get. I am going to send you a note when I get back and give you some more of what I have taken away here; is that alright?"

"Absolutely, and please know this was no imposition. I am honored that you shared this all with me. I hope you will also realize that even with this short conversation and what we just shared, that's what makes relationships magical. Leaders know their people and are there for their people. Just as each of us wants and appreciates our leader being there for us, hearing us, supporting us. It has everything to do with what we are preaching and teaching here; especially what that Relate breakout session was all about.

Debra, consider how this applies to you and those you lead. What could happen if you had an open relationship with your folks and they were also close to all those they work with? What if you could talk to them like you just spoke to me, nearly a stranger? When relationship is strong, so is everything else.

I just heard this all reinforced on a radio talk show yesterday, heading to something over the noon hour. Don't know if you know Dave Ramsey, the Christian speaker, radio host, who helps people get out of debt, do you?"

Seeing her smile and acknowledge she followed him as well, "He is also big on leadership, and yesterday he was kind of preaching on workplace relations and managing folks. He was saying something to the effect that he wouldn't have someone he wasn't a friend with on his team; just going on about the importance of relationship, people enjoying their work, the people there, you the boss and all that. Good stuff, he and I are completely on track in that sense. Listen, now it's me taking your time. Okay, you better go. Take care, and I will be looking for that note once you get back. Hey by the way, let's talk after the wrap up session this afternoon, take my business card, there's my cell number, call me if we get lost in the crowd. I would like to meet your boss as well if he's around."

"You guys are going to come and share this with the CEO, the senior leadership and our company sometime soon; you have to," she was off, smiling and waving at him as she rounded the corner.

Before returning, Debra stopped by the conference's travel agency table to confirm their ride to the airport tonight. She discovered the lady's name there was the same as hers. Within minutes, both were sitting and discovered some other life connections. Discovering both had been at dinner last night, this included their faith and God. They exchanged numbers; Debra was to call her to confirm the time they wished to depart

VIP TRAVELINKS

*Call us for all of your conference
or other business travel plans!
We can also plan your next vacation!*

Deb Stafford-Gray
913.334.5302
Viptravelinks@yahoo.com

Please use this page for notes.

Breakout Session #7: Accommodate

The facilitator, from Hawaii with accent, skin complexion and plenty of pride in her culture to match, was leading this session.

"Aloha, my friends." After talking a bit about herself, education, experience and her heritage, along with sharing her passion for leadership and management work, she kicked off the discussion. "Let me get us rolling, gesturing at the slide on the wall; this Support & Shield bullet is something that seems to get a lot of discussion.

As the leader of your people, it is your duty and responsibility to lead and care for them in every way. One of those aspects is to realize that these are nobody's people, as in nobody...but yours. No one has the right to come mess with them, give them direction, change things or any other sort of business and/or operational interaction. Leaders accommodate all; relate and network with all; welcome and work with all internal customers; but still support and shield yours, those you lead."

Mark, a VP from a small company in Illinois jumped in, "This is interesting. Let me challenge this a bit; how about the CEO coming down, doing that MBWA and changing something? This is kind of big and a popular thing we do in our culture." She was smiling with a sort of smirk on her face. "This happens all the time in our organization; the CEO, VPs, and other upper managers do this sort of thing. We have always viewed it as a good thing."

"Here's the thing, another set of eyes is always a good thing; but how things observed is dealt with is the point here. Conceptually, all leaders should respect this support and shield idea or thinking with any and all leaders in the organization." The Aloha-Lady as she quickly became referred to had responded and continued, "These are not the CEO's people, or his or her team, are they?"

Without much pause she answered her own question, "For the record, our point of view here at the Great 8 is the answer is no. After all the CEO only really leads his or her VPs or senior leadership staff; their immediate and direct reports. This is something people struggle with a bit, but there is a need for every leader from the CEO down through the most junior supervisor to grasp this idea. When real leadership takes hold in an organization, leaders mutually get this and respect it. You being a VP, you do realize that the people below you are not all yours either, right?

Sure, to cut off some of the potential arguments and move on as quickly as possible here ...we can all agree that the CEO is responsible for the entire organization.

However, once again, this responsibility should include the responsibility of creating a real leadership-oriented chain of command and leadership team. If he/she or some other senior manager changes something, what does it say about that individual's actual immediate supervisor or leader?

This CEO or senior leader leads, grows, coaches, mentors, develops relationships which evaluates, communicates and all these great eight concepts with their team. If he or she wishes to communicate something to someone or get something changed, it should go through the chain of command. That person, area, function or department affected should get it from their own leader! We realize most of your companies may not be doing this very well. Still it is how an effective leadership team practices leadership. Is this making sense?"

Following a bit of discussion, they pretty much reached a consensus on this being how things *should* work. Some were still struggling with the idea a bit. Some follow-up discussions after the conference were agreed upon by the few stewing about it.

Debra raising her hand to get attention, "I'd like to hit on this enabling idea. Before yesterday and specifically before hearing about this teaching fishing concept, I might have had some trouble with this enabling thing. We enable when we solve problems; when we don't hold people accountable; hand them fish; tell people what to do, and so forth. As my boss would toss in here, we enable when I micro-manage my people!"

Jack, in the back retorted, "I am amazed once again, at just how overlapping and connected so much of this leadership stuff really is. So many dynamics are so intertwined within all eight of these Great 8 principles. I like Debra there, thought and actually was pretty sure coming that this conference was all just some marketing, newest and greatest, money-making consultant's scheme. I believe you guys really have done a decent job of capturing and conveying the dynamics relevant to real leadership; kudos to you guys. This is a just a great way to encompass and capture true leadership; not management, but leadership. I'm just saying," he smiled and stood to continue a point he wanted to address.

"What I wanted to mention was something I ran across a long while back about this time management thing. At some point yesterday, one of us shared about that monkey concept thing – taking monkeys on our back, obviously affecting our time management. That was so right on and ties into time management, delegation, and so on. What I have gathered about delegation over time tells me that it is probably the biggest time management key or tip out there. It is a concept that should be understood and fully utilized by leaders at all levels; but more often than not it is misunderstood and poorly executed.

It obviously ties to that talk we just had on the CEO or some other senior official walking around; sometimes they take on these monkeys unknowingly."

Alicia stood applauding briefly, "Well said Jack, that so happens to take us into another area. If I may, here's my take on the value of delegating. If it is practiced well, on the front end, it can be a very time consuming skill. It becomes a real time saver and value only in the long run, after you have developed and trained your people ...through effective delegation! Also delegating develops two-way trust, that you trusted me to do this and that I know you can be trusted to get the job done.

Delegation develops people to be better prepared to do higher-level work. It develops thinking skills, problem solving abilities, initiative, confidence, and self-esteem. It also allows you to discover strengths and weaknesses of your people. Consider this scenario...by delegating, I am developing that person to take on more responsibility and allowing me time to practice leadership in other areas. If I take advantage of this opportunity, I can also become a better coach to those that I have delegated to, since I will have to do some coaching along the way. The challenge is not to do too much and get in the way...after all; too much coaching can signal a lack of trust.

When you delegate, and to your second bullet up there, we need to be available; there may be questions and issues that come up."

Robin tossed in the following before Alicia or anyone else reacted, "Good, you are right on there, my friend, and I'll give you another huge point! Regardless of the outcome, the responsibility of the delegated action remains with you. If it goes well, the person who did the work gets the credit; if it doesn't go so well—guess who gets the blame? That's right, we, the leader are still accountable and responsible. This piece is crucial to your ability to gain buy-in to the whole idea of delegation. What I mean here is that one of the killers to delegating is the risk aspect. You must take the risk out of the equation for them - the only real risk here is the one that you are taking, by delegating. From personal experience here's another tip - it is a good idea to bring your own boss into the thought-process when delegating. You want to ensure in some cases that your boss realizes and buys into the idea of taking *this risk with that* person. You may discover that this particular action or project is one that the boss does not want you to risk."

Aloha-Lady stepped back into, "And by practicing real delegation, in the process of doing so, you learn more about delegation, coaching, relationship-building, developing people, etc."

She paused momentarily for effect, taking a breath, then continued on, "And to identify strengths, utilize resources effectively, support, praise and on and on and on…as well as improved trust.

Who knows, with enough of this, properly done, you may actually get a day off some day! I learned way too late in my own leadership career the true value of delegation. By finally utilizing this skill and art, it allowed me time to do what I truly wanted and needed to be doing. It allows me to be out there among the people I was leading and developing those relationships. It all goes round and round and round, the value of it all.

See how everything with leadership supports and reinforces other leadership stuff my friends? Whoever just said it, yes these Great 8 principles are so intertwined, reinforcing and tied into the others."

Some good points were made following up on this topic. Several minutes of conversation on other topics were fitted in as well. Then just as the facilitator was getting set to go to the next bullet, someone interrupted.

"This all sounds so much like Servant Leadership. Like the bullet up there about supporting and shielding.   You serve them and support your people's needs in doing their job; or maybe even helping them with personal issues. After all, what they do or don't do is what is going to make or break you.   We need to know what they need and facilitate getting them the support and resources they need to succeed at their job. I have always been a big proponent of Servant Leadership and for sure the eight principles here are all about the serving dynamic...another big wow for me!" Robin had thrown this in with an increasingly excited tone as she spoke.

Aloha Lady was nodding and agreeing with all said; then led into another bullet, "Participating in all directions, our last bullet up there; let me tell you what we mean by this. This is about discovering all of our internal customers, peers, other management folks that support my team, department and/or function. Establishing relationships right from the beginning is key to a manager's success. It is possible that people and players around your world, have a past history and maybe even some baggage regarding your team, department or function you are managing.

You probably have already heard this in another breakout, but it's worth repeating. Go have a cup of coffee, listen, accommodate and discover what the issues and challenges he or she might have had with your team in the past. In the beginning they have nothing on you yet anyway; so develop these relationships and bridges strongly before the issues do come out. Make sense? It's about accommodating people in all directions around us; that are what leaders do. They find time to deal with other's concerns, their needs, help they require, they service them and they work with them to resolve things. That's accommodation my friends!"

The lady next to Debra raised her hand suggesting, "Something this reminds me of, well, I learned a little while back is that when I have issues, conflicts and bad relationships with my peers... This causes conflicts, issues and poor relationships down below as well. Think on this for a moment. Here's an example that occurred as I was supervising a few shift leaders a while back. I had two subordinate leaders; a Day Shift Supervisor and the Night Time Supervisor who didn't get along. This was known by all below and filtered down and played out in dynamics down below. Guess who else didn't get along? Their people, the day shift would leave issues for the night shift and vice versa. This began happening a lot, and it went on and on and on. They know that this is unsolvable and are totally frustrated because of their boss's issues with your boss.

To me this dynamic ties into this accommodation thing. I need to accommodate the other shift supervisor and vice versa? You get my point here? The fighting and problems were escalating and they would just continue to fight and bicker. It was solved only when I began working on their relationships with each other; which by the way was my job. This is not just about these kinds of shift situations; it goes on throughout organizations between departments, between execs, between silos that emerge, etc. My boss doesn't like your boss, so I don't have to like and work with you either, nah, nah, nah. Been there done this haven't you? This insanity happens, trust me and believe me. Anyone seen it happen?"

As Aloha Lady was thanking her, the Connections sheets were getting passed around.

Accommodate: Great 8 Connections & 'food for thought'…

Notice how the other seven concepts support, reinforce, and connect with this one.

DEMONSTRATE   …receptiveness / availability to new people, ideas, and so on—model.

COMMUNICATE   …with everyone, openly—sharing and receiving information.

RELATE   …relationships are built when we discover and avail ourselves to others.

EVALUATE   …constantly assess awareness and accessibility—you and yours.

CREATE   …an environment of creating—accommodating improves creativity.

ELIMINATE   …resolve blocks and hindrances; listen to and hear everyone.

FACILITATE   …the time taken to really process the information you've just been open to.

<u>Please make your own notes and comments below.</u>

There was a barrage of comments and examples; many were tied back to the last topic and emotions the friend of Debra's had sparked. There were more than a couple of people confessing they had been one of these leaders causing just these sorts of issues themselves.

> # ACCOMMODATE:
> ## ...to be of service!
>
> ## "Are you serving those you lead?"

The Aloha Lady clicking the remote bringing up a new slide began wrapping up "I hope you have seen the light with this accommodating piece. Being accommodating, has a deep meaning for leaders. This requires a lot of careful digging and understanding to really get the learning here; I believe your comments and stories have helped me expose most of it. I would say it is a whole lot about the concept of Servant Leadership. I would also urge you to think of what Booker spoke to in the opening session yesterday; that natural leader thing? If you now picture that individual, and think of this dynamic; my bet is you will agree that he or she is an accommodating leader?" The facilitator let it soak in while she strolled all the way around the room and group.

She abruptly grabbed their attention back, "Am I accommodating by giving answers? Am I accommodating when I look over their shoulder, when I micro-manage? What about taking those monkeys, seems like it to some degree doesn't it?   What about not delegating? And what about not developing strong relationships that affect them, those that I am leading? That was a great discussion, gang. Feel free to call me if I can ever help in your world. Enjoy your last session and I'll see you at the wrap up in a little while."

Debra's Notes about ROI after Breakout #7

Consequences of Disengagement:

- Increased turnover
- Missed deadlines
- Low morale
- Increased worker's compensation claims
- Higher absenteeism
- Call-ins and No-shows
- Lack of accountability
- Lack of responsibility
- Disregard for compliance and regulations
- Gossip and conflict
- Low retention of high performers

....do some follow-up figuring, but disengagement has to be costing us/me; maybe impacting productivity: 7-12%?

I know I have had disengagement with some of my staff and that it's costing the company a lot of money.

I was skeptical, but now I'm a convert. However, I'm still keenly aware that the company is not progressive in its investment in training programs unless they proved to be absolutely necessary. *A major discussion with a business case to support my position is needed.

Please use this page for notes.

Breakout Session #8: Demonstrate

Demonstrate

- Model and Example
- Teaching and Learning
- Respect of Values
- The VISION
- Relationships!!!
- Professionalism
- Okay to be Wrong

On each seat there was a handout that Debra and a few others in the group had seen before. It had seemed pretty cool, but now it seemed to carry a much deeper meaning. Katy the facilitator had also put up a slide of the handout up on the screen.

Over the course of the breakout session, all would discover Katy was this cool lady from Colorado; she was also a Corporate Trainer for some big bank. She was a leader with personality to match. Booker had taught her in a graduate class a few years back, and afterward sought her out to help in many respects with the conference.

> **You "can't not" lead by example!**
>
> Think about it!
>
> I would rather **see** a sermon than **hear** one any day!
>
> I'd rather you would walk with me, than merely show me the way.
>
> The lectures you deliver may be very wise and true, but I think I'll get my lesson by **watching what you do**!
>
> I might misunderstand you, and all the advice you give but *there's no misunderstanding how you act and how you live.*
>
> **We are always leading by example!**
>
> Think about it!

As Debra read this, she thought about all that had been covered these last two days. She pondered and wondered to herself 'how do I model all this stuff'? She grinned to herself, thinking it made a lot of sense to have this as the last learning session; how do we model all of the previous seven?

She also thought how can we be modeling all of this good stuff, these principles all the time? Raising her hand, standing and moving off to a side wall to lean against; she posed the question to the group.

Immediately some hands went up and Janae didn't wait but offered, "I think this is all about why we have to have that open and trusting relationship, that culture developed of being alright with being wrong. We cannot really know for sure we are modeling all the right things. It is about realizing we need other's input and feedback to hold us accountable to change our own behavior; without it we are blindly doing our job.

Am I on track here? I really don't see how we can just believe we are doing all this and assume so. I guess that's what I have been doing for a number of years, now that I think of it. I'm kind of betting that's what most managers do; just believe they are leading effectively?"

This caused some nodding, lots of chattering, and side conversations. There was a lot of open back and forth jabs, sarcasm and challenging of each other. This was all on the increase likely due to this being the last session; the group had bonded in a strong and enjoyable way. Some lasting friendships had developed and would sustain as it turned out.

Kenisha stood and made her way next to Debra against the side wall, walking backward to see all, she began, "This *Demonstrate* topic was for sure a great one to be our last session. Everything we have talked about for two days is what this is all about? If we are doing all these things, all within the great eight concepts, we must be modeling the right stuff surely?"

The room had grown noisy. Debra, obviously into some deep thought, evidenced by her facial expression and tone; broke in, "Oh my gosh! This just struck me. I was sitting here struggling not being able to hear, because all of you, I mean all of us were carrying on our side conversations. It just hit me about this demonstrating thing and what we were doing here, a bunch of leaders, what were we demonstrating talking all over each other? I am thinking now of how bad I am about doing just that, chattering with someone next to me in meetings back at my company. As the slide says there, we *cannot not* be leading by example …every freaking thing we do is being watched.

What am I modeling, demonstrating, and practicing as a leader? Yikes. I wasn't trying to be ugly with you guys here, please forgive. I just had to share that, so much is coming to light for me. I wonder how much bad stuff we all practice and model in our routines."

Katy smiling, looked straight at Debra, then gazed around the room at all, "Glad that didn't get past us Debra; likely I don't need to add on to that, great point. And thanks Kenisha, you are precisely right, it is indeed a great point, how *do* we know? Of course the answer should be we can only know through others; our boss, being coached, mentored, corrected, our behaviors noticed, and so on. We have to give that permission to others to help us know. On top of that, involving those around us to help us know when we are practicing some bad behavior."

The lady who had sat next to Debra throughout was back into the flow, "What it makes me think about which I have been doing for most of last night and today is that we can't just model. We have to teach as well. Yes, we have to model the right stuff; we need to do that for sure. But also then talk to it, teach it, preach it. I think about my boss who practices some of this so well. I guess now that I think about it, he was messing up, not holding me accountable to be practicing all this. At least not all of it, or maybe I just have been blowing him off about a lot of it?" She was smiling and jotting this down to remember to dog him later.

This led to many comments, confessions, accusations and observations about each other's bosses. There were some who modeled the wrong thing, some who were built up as being awesome. Most self reflected that they had much room for improvement in this area, modeling and setting the right example for anyone and everyone.

A good 15 minutes of dialogue came to an end as Katy broke in, "I really appreciate the honesty here you guys. It does no good for us to do otherwise," the facilitator walked over and grabbed a sheet of paper from a stack of materials. "I read something a couple of days ago that I wanted to share, and it fits here pretty well.

I was reading an interview in the McKinsey Quarterly, a great resource for leaders by the way. It was a March 2011 article, 'Flying people, not planes', by the CEO of Bombardier, a Canadian company on building a world-class culture. Bear with me just a moment; a few lines from interview were something like, I think you will get the points and context as I paraphrase a bit here.

'Everyone in management recognized we had a problem but insisted it wasn't in their department... At the management level, there were cultural problems too... The culture was about avoiding putting facts on the table. We would go to a leadership forum and spend three days telling each other why we were good. If a person brought up a problem, someone else would say words like yes, but you did not really understand the issue properly; we're actually really good. It was a culture of not facing up to issues, of blaming other departments, and so on.'

"That's probably enough to make the point; and by the way you might want to go read the whole interview. As I read the article I thought to myself, WOW, is this so real. We rarely go into an organization to help with their leadership and/or people-system, where we do not initially have to help them break through this dynamic described in this interview! We spend a lot time upfront, which we have to; to break this down before we can do any good.

We have to more or less say directly words like yes obviously you are good and have strengths, but we are here to improve, address weaknesses and get better. Let's stop fooling ourselves, lying to each other, or being defensive.

The trust needed among upper levels of management is frequently just not there, making this a hurdle to first get over. When the leadership gets it, understands this, and really begins focusing on them—then and only then can amazing improvement begin to happen.

The question for you the manager, the CEO, the HR Champion, or any of us is: Are you ready to really make a positive difference in your organization, or will we just keep telling ourselves everything is fine? When all else fails, try addressing leadership!

Well, you get it, huh? We can only learn, grow and get better when we become aware. So a question to you all right here, right now; are you maybe at least more aware after these last two days?"

Lots of smiles, applause, and agreement took place within the room. Katy continued, "Good stuff, thanks, good to hear. We're about done here. With this being your last breakout, we are pretty free to go anywhere here in these last ten minutes or so, as long as it is somewhat connected. So what's on your minds? Anyone have anything different, or any more follow-up from what we have been speaking to for the last hour or so?"

Several hands went up with Jack just going for it, not waiting to be picked, "Well under the assumption it was part of our discussion here, I'll bring some focus to the handout in our packet. "This top eight thing" he said, waving it in the air for all to see, "it's pretty interesting stuff."

1. I want my boss to support me, shield me, and care about me (not just care about what I can do on the job).
2. I wish that my boss would deal with that one person who makes everybody else miserable. That one "bad apple" is just allowed to do whatever they want because they are afraid of them, or think that we can't live without them. What a joke.
3. I want to be involved early on regarding impending changes, new ideas, and solutions to problems. When I'm not involved, I don't care very much about how well things are done — I become very apathetic.
4. I need the opportunity to develop myself, learn new skills, be promoted, or even just recognized for what I do now.
5. I wish my boss with communicate with me about what's going on, not just about what they think I need to know. I find out more from coworkers than from my boss.
6. I want conflict to be dealt with fairly and quickly. When people are in conflict, it is allowed to fester, which drives everyone else crazy and puts everyone on edge.
7. I need my boss to provide me with the resources necessary to do my job well.
8. I wish I were more challenged and that more work was delegated to me. My boss is afraid to let anyone else do anything for fear of looking incompetent, or maybe my boss just doesn't trust anyone. How will we every get any better like this?

A voice arose, not heard much at all over the two days. "It seems apparent to me that this ties into our vision, our goals, and what we ought to try to model. It is also part of what we should evaluate leaders on, if we are being honest and really trying to improve leaders and leadership. If we could be all this, which I am sure we all want in our own boss as well, we would be one awesome leader wouldn't we?" Sherrie, from the St. Louis area had tossed in; one of just a couple of words she had said over the two days.

Katy jumped back in somewhat repeating some of Sherrie's ideas;, challenging and asking for other's input to Sherrie's words and thoughts.

The woman next to Debra, her new friend in a very low tone spoke, "You know I cannot get away from something mentioned here somewhere in the last couple of days, that slogan 'People, Our Most Valuable Resource'. This has been over our HR Manager's office door for well at least the nine years I have been there. Rarely however does it really play out in our walk and actions there! Our employees, the people must see it as just talk, as the phrasing goes. With all I have heard these last two days, I would have to admit, my personal leader-walk has been pretty flawed as well."

Debra had clearly evolved into one of the most vocal members of the group. She picked up here, "That was awesome for you to acknowledge my new buddy; and I will second it. I too have been pretty dang flawed as well. When you stop and really think about it, as we have these two days, it's so stupid. Business and organizations just really don't get do they? People, and I might add leaders, are definitively the most valuable resource of any company.

For real, our most valuable resource is more pointedly the leadership. The leaders of our most valuable resource are the most under-utilized and most under-developed, in practice. I'm sitting here thinking; consider for a moment, all the other resources within our organizations. Time, money, inventory, operations, machinery, facilities, systems and processes; they get all the real focus. I know I'm just rambling a bit here, but think how much effort is put in to managing *those*. We do preventive maintenance, planning and organizing, fixing, training, repairing, replacing, etc. We tend to be pretty proactive regarding other resources. We wouldn't hesitate for a moment to discover waste, find solutions and put in overtime hours to fix other stuff. However when it comes to people, it is pretty much all reactive, all just assuming, accepting of just the way things are, the way they have to be, and so forth.

We react or don't ...to people's behaviors, performance issues, conflicts, lack of team skills, development, etc. But we really never systematically address solutions or fixes in a sustainable way in our people-system."

Looking directly at the facilitator, she continued without pause, "This Eight Great group, or at least the principles, the learning; we need you or it in our company. We have got to get you there, or in some way, we have to use this information to get our leaders fixed. And yes that means me as well. We have to begin modeling, demonstrating the right stuff, teaching, accommodating, all this!"

Several people seconded and *thirded* the thought, as Sherrie blurted out from the back wall, "You are so right, and I second that as well, we need all this brought into our business as well. We have to figure out leadership and start growing leaders and leadership. I must tell you, I am also going to try to apply this at home in my parenting, as well as talk to my pastor about; our church leadership could sure use all this."

Katy responded, "Well you have no idea what it means to hear you all validating what we have developed; what we teach! We would obviously be happy to speak to any organization here and be there if we could work that out. However, let me challenge each of you; how do you fix you, yourself? Assuming even if your organization were to begin some process, that will take time, what could you as a leader do right now regarding all this?"

There was a long pause, the facilitator allowed the silence to go on. Debra and others were looking at their notes, some looking up into the air thinking. Debra flipped some pages and scanned her notes, "Well, I will tell you what I have captured and think about regarding fixing me. It was mentioned somewhere in one of our sessions about how we have expectations, job descriptions, etc for any and every job in our organization, except when it comes to managers. It seems to me, and will tell you what I'm going to do, when I get back. I'm sitting down with Les, my boss, the COO, the CEO and all; we are going to establish a set of leadership competencies, maybe something tied closely to these great eight concepts, qualities, traits, skills, etc. I'm going to also involve my own team in developing these; what do they want in me, etc. Then we have to start defining them and coaching each other to begin changing behavior and practicing real leadership stuff?" she paused looking around and after a brief pause and realizing they seemed open for her to finish, she continued.

"Well, it is again just like any job, we set expectations, standards and then do routine feedback and performance coaching until we are satisfied they are doing the job right. We have to beginning with the top; do the same thing with leadership, management, supervision, etc. We have to start growing leadership, as Susan and others here have said."

The Arkansas participant chimed in for just the second time, "Good stuff y'all. That's my Arkansas lingo, saying y'all; it pops up now and then. Since we're onto that, do you all know what the plural of y'all is?" After just a moment, he responded, "all y'all! Sorry couldn't resist, pretty lame but just had to share that; more Geography learning maybe?"

Plenty of laughter followed, as the facilitator picked back up, "Nice y'all! Now back to the topic here, fixing you. Debra and some of the rest of you just put out some good thinking. In addition, the answers as to how to do this have all been covered over these last two days. Please trust what is in your materials packets and the content within these Great Eight concepts as a whole bunch to help and maybe even *the* answer.

At least to our way of thinking here ...what organizations, business and companies never quite get is that we must establish a target, a set of leadership accountabilities and competencies. Then they have to become everything everywhere, in our hiring of leaders and even people overall; part of performance assessment, not just their technical, business stuff but all these other traits, practices, qualities and expectations we should have for leaders to practice."

Robin slipped into the dialogue, "I don't know where I'm going here, but I guess I just want to say thanks for opening my eyes and giving me plenty to focus on. The content of the breakouts as well as all that you guys have shared has helped me immensely. It is all about the people, our most valuable resource. This means from the top leader with that team, and every level or layer of leadership and every leader doing their job as a leader. Man we are messing up at my company. I'll stop blabbing, I'm done. I really am done now; I can cram no more into this brain of mine!"

Debra's buddy chimed back in, "It hasn't been mentioned, but I guess this Professionalism bullet up there, is maybe the compilation of all this isn't it? Modeling and practicing all these eight great things, we would become well, a professional leader I think. I guess that makes all of us amateurs right now doesn't it? It seems to me that it is also about appearance, how we carry ourselves, language, our personality maybe, how we speak, how we treat folks, how we are seen by others, etc. Wow this is kind of a tricky one the more I think of it.   Can we measure it as a leadership competency?" She was looking over at Debra for the most part as she stopped.

"What are you looking at me for, I don't know," Debra responded with a huge smile. Jack grabbed onto the question, without much prompting, "I suspect we all could sit here and define it and what all it could be, but then again, that's the point, we must define all of these. The organization, the people, the management need to reach consensus and just start working on them, defining them and gaining clarity along the way. Yes, that would be the way it seems. After all, in answer to your question, we absolutely can measure and judge it; we do it all the time. I suspect to make a point; we have all been looking at people for the last two days, and judging them. All of us have looked at someone for some reason and judged them not very professional. We all do this with others all the time; we need to just start doing it in a way that makes a difference, by telling people out loud. We should stop talking to others about others, but rather make it part of performance counseling, and ultimately our culture!" He paused, nearly out of breath, looking back at the lady who had obviously become a friend to all, "That was pretty good wasn't it ... how did I do?"

The lady, then Katy, then all started smiling and applauding. Robin now standing in the back, yelled out, "From some movie many years ago, there was a famous line, 'by George, I think you've got it' or something like that. Wait a minute, or maybe, that Field of Dreams line, 'Build it and he will come'."

Katy waited for things to calm down a bit, and summarized the bullets with some different twists in about five minutes or so. He then concluded as he clicked the remote, "Since it is right there in front of me, I will tag onto Robin's line there about building; Booker's second book is titled Rebuilding on Rock, and I would strongly urge you to give it a read.

One more time, it is Connections time. Will someone hand these out as I just quickly make mention of a few items that hopefully will put the icing on the cake regarding how these all connect. I'm sure I don't need to say too much, because by George, I do think you all get it."

Demonstrate: Great 8 Connections & 'food for thought'...

Notice how the other seven concepts support, reinforce, and connect with this one.

COMMUNICATE   ...professional, open, tactful, productive, and respectful interactions.

RELATE   ...growing productive relationships with people, networks, and customers.

EVALUATE   ...expectations, trust, and accountability—constantly.

CREATE   ...create an environment in which people continually strive to improve and better themselves.

ELIMINATE   ...the acceptance of bad practices such as waste, failure, and irresponsibility.

FACILITATE   ...effective modeling at all times to produce results.

ACCOMMODATE   ...behaviors model leadership—demand leadership in others.

Please make your own notes and comments below.

Now, I have to get you guys gone, so we can all be at the wrap up session, in let's see about eight minutes. We nearly always find a way to leave folks with this quote which you have seen already, but maybe now it carries even more significance. We use what we believe is John Maxwell's quoted a lot around here.

> "People don't care how much you KNOW until they first know how much you CARE.
> (We give credit to John Maxwell for this quote.)
>
> "…and when leaders effectively practice the Great Eight Principles, your people will KNOW that you CARE."

God bless you each; my prayers are with you as you head out and the Good Lord willing will have a safe trip home. We are all at the other end of a phone call if we can ever answer any questions or help you. For leaders who attend these conferences, we keep an open door or phone line for you to return, contact us, seek us out for resources, etc. Hope to see you all again someday soon. Again, safe travels and take very good care my new friends!"

Debra's Notes about ROI after Breakout #8

Excited now and need to maintain that enthusiasm. With a little additional research upon return, I will be enthusiastic!

I need to put the concepts to work immediately as well as plan for the transformations that WILL occur in my sphere of influence within the organization.

The most important thing to start with is modeling the behaviors I expect of other people—become an example they can follow, every minute, every day. As Les, my peers, and MY TEAM to told me accountable.

Once I establish trust, I need to start teaching others about learning together as a team.

TASK for self—once a week, go out and work WITH THEM for an hour in production, side by side. The time invested should produce a tenfold (10x) return in credibility, with my staff, understanding of issues, and most importantly gaining more and more of my team's trust and building relationships.

There will be many challenges with this modified approach, but I am confident that, along with my business case and ROI calculations, that my team and organization will reap excellent benefits.

NOW, how can I implement these changes into my personal life, as well? ☺

NOTE TO SELF: Relationship = ROI

Please use this page for notes.

Final Wrap-up Session

Booker is down on the floor among the people as the place fills up for the Wrap-Up/Closing session.   Robin from KC is bending his ear about anything and everything, carrying on what a great conference it has been. Just then he spotted Debra that Booker had met a few hours ago. They made some quick introductions with Les and Mickey, as Booker excused himself heading up the stairs to kick things off for the closing session.

At the same time, Raul follows him up on the stage down at the far end; waving with both arms for the other facilitators to join them. They come up from different directions, high fiving some participants, slapping each other on the back, shaking hands, exchanging a few hugs, etc. You get the picture.

The Aloha Lady moves toward the podium grabbing a mike, "Aloha, welcome back, greetings, we are so glad you are still here and didn't leave," she says jokingly with the crowd all smiling and responding with some laughter. She continues, "We are up here just to summarize, wrap up and restate a point or two you have heard us make over the last few days about leadership. We are modeling a learning point right now; we really like each other, and we even like the boss. And we are pretty sure he likes us as well, huh ol' great boss of ours?"

She was getting a positive affirmation nod and thumbs up from Booker as Raul grabbed the mike, "Now don't get us wrong here, because this isn't just some learning technique. We really do socialize and really are friends. We really do like each other, we really do go out and have a good time together, and we work together, play together and enjoy it. And we really do set high expectations and hold each other accountable as well. For me personally, at least for me, I love these guys," he looked over at the others who were smiling, high fiving some more, giving him the thumbs up; as he continued.

"So did you learn anything? How about the skeptics are you still here or did you leave?"

Katy, one of the facilitators, taking the mike asked, "So are you still skeptical, did we make any headway regarding that skepticism?" Katy walked out in front to seek responses. Many people raised their hands, and comments came out from the audience, "...still here.......you didn't get rid of me yet....I get it, I am converted, etc..."

As the facilitators walked across to the end of the stage, heading as a group down the stairs, Booker was slowly moving to the podium. As he sipped his bottle of water, he waited watching the group interacting with the people at the end of each aisle and accepting even more high fives. He was all psyched up, *miked* up, free of being locked to the podium.

"Aloha, everyone!" He hollered as the crowd responded back with various other language and cultural greetings.

"Okay, so we are here, near the end. As was just said, that's the absolute truth. You may have heard this from someone already, but just as I have heard Dave Ramsey say, I do not either want to work with someone who is not also a friend.

We are like a really solid tightly knit family; not the dysfunctional one you came from; sorry maybe I shouldn't have gone there, huh?" he was pointing and smiling as the crowd laughed almost in unison. "We are close, I am their boss and buddy and they are mine. It really can work you skeptics; and FYI, when you create it, and build it, powerful results will come from those efforts. Trust me.

I know I am speaking for all of us here at the Great Eight Conference; this has been our pleasure and a blast. You see, it is truly an honor for us to be able to share our learning with you. Not only do *we* get to meet a bunch of neat folks, so do we. We always meet just prior to this Wrap-up session, over the lunch hour briefly as we did again today. You wouldn't believe me anyway, you will think I say that to all groups; but this has been one of our best conferences ever. Don't let me burst your bubble, but in fact this is nearly always the case, every conference! You see, we don't just take just anyone to these; there is a bit of screening and qualifying. As you know, well unless you were directed to be here..." he paused to smile, chuckle and mess with the group a bit. "We do a bit of investigating why people want to attend. It is part of why this just works, because we understood and assured ourselves that we could meet your expectations. You were motivated to be here, to learn, or someone thought enough of you to get you here.

Now, before we wrap things up, something we always try to do is seek out someone who we feel has benefited here maybe a bit more than anyone. This is not always easy, and I'm sure we don't always get the right one in this sense; however this time it's a slam dunk. I know we have picked someone who has truly gained and will no doubt take real leadership understanding, ROI and a readiness to teach, back with her. She knows nothing of this, so please be easy on her. Will Debra from Seattle come up here?"

The spotlight searched and was on her immediately as they had already determined where she was and Booker was pointing at her, gesturing for her to come up. Debra was to say the least shocked, and not all that willing to get up, but Les and Mickey basically shoved her, pushing her from her seat. She really had little choice.

As Debra came forward, Booker was explaining, "Debra actually caused this and did it to herself, didn't you Debra?" he was looking at her coming up the stairs and smiling hugely. She was remembering her talk this morning and realized why he had called her out. She was nodding positively and timidly; she got it.

Booker grabbed Debra around the shoulders, pulling her close to him as she arrived next to him. He was handed a microphone by Raul for Debra to use, as he escorted her together toward the front center of the stage.

"So, Debra, what do you think?" Booker smiled, some remarks and chuckles arose from the audience as he continued, "Now I had to put in another plug for my books didn't I? Of course that's my teaching fishing instinct coming out. Sincerely, as the leader here, on a serious note, I want to truly know what you think first. For those of you who don't know, Debra was one of those skeptics up front; making this a great pick, at least for me!

So Debra I'm not really going to help you out much here; what do you think?" Booker handed her the mike as he stepped back, whispering to her to share what she shared with him this morning.

It took Debra a bit of time to get it out, but along with some tears, she conjured up some words to express her feelings and thoughts. She told the group how much she really needed this. She conveyed how much she had not been caring for her people, much less about them and their problems. She even dabbled in how her divorce and all that had impacted her and her leadership.

She was a different person, from not only what she learned here, but what she heard from those friends she had made here. She did end with, "FYI, I am ...or was, one of those skeptics which have been dogged from the beginning of the conference," she said as she looked back pointing at Booker and then out at his facilitator group. "You guys do have a grip on all this. I think that's what made it all work for me, you understand leaders, managers, supervisors, etc. You get the skepticism, the dilemma, the lack of development we get, why it happens and all that leadership stuff we need; but don't just naturally possess. For me anyway, thanks for opening my eyes my friends."

Just then, Les raises his hand and rises without really any acknowledgement, "For those of you here, I am Debra's servant, I mean boss. Booker, you have no idea who you have converted here. You have no idea...well maybe you do, but let me just tell you that Debra there was pretty darned upset about being sent here. For you guys to win her over, well, my hat's off to you guys. Going through it all myself, I can also tell you, I was not a skeptic, but I have learned a ton.

If I may, I am also wondering about bringing the Great 8 principles and your training in to our company; you guys do that right? I know the answer is yes and I'm also guessing, being the money guy, the CFO at our company, what that's going to cost us. I am also sure that Debra and I can convince the boss of the ROI and will get you out to see us very soon! I'll sit down but again thanks for not only what I have learned but for fixing Debra!...who I never quite could convince about this leadership thing!" he was laughing and pointing at her as he sat down.

Booker briefly stepped forward responding a bit about Debra; also acknowledged that they could work with any companies here, and would try to help in any way they could. He said pricing rarely was an issue if the situation was right, and the potential was good for truly helping. He allowed Debra to struggle through a few more words, after handing her a couple of tissues for the tears. They exchanged a big hug as he escorted her down the stairs.

Turning to address everyone again, backing up the stairs, he said, "Before I forget, let's not miss a learning opportunity here before kicking you all out of here. Remember yesterday in this same room, I asked you all who had an attitude. So how many are still here with that same attitude, with that same skepticism, and so on?" He paused, gladly seeing no hands going up. "Listen I realize there may be a few of you that are still not completely bought in; I just hope you not raising your hand does indeed indicate that you have changed your mind a bit anyway. I will assume that at least a fair amount of awareness has set in, and you at least want to understand more.

So, just a bit more on this point, just so it doesn't get by us. Why did we have that attitude? Because we were directed, not involved, and therefore had no buy-in. This is a huge concept to realize for leaders; maybe even humongous, if there is such a word. Real leaders are always dealing with change, and facilitating that change involves dynamics that don't result in these kinds of attitudes. When we are forced, directed, had it crammed down our throats, we are going to resist. Just as you resisted, so will your people when you try to implement change without their buy-in, their ownership, their acceptance, their understanding, etc. As we mentioned at various points during our breakouts, this applies to all areas of leadership as well.

This applies to whatever level of skepticism you may still have; challenge yourself to get it, to truly understand study and buy-in. Only then will you really internalize and pursue continual improvement in you and this leadership stuff!

On another side of this, parents, any of you out there? Is there a message there for you, the leaders in the household? Obviously yes, and I'm not challenging your parenting skills here; just making a connection hopefully. When we respond to the kid who asks the why question ...with your old worthless because I said so, it just doesn't fly. Resistance occurs, doesn't it?

Just because you are in charge, it still just doesn't sell well. Real leaders get this dynamic and that includes all of us in parenting, coaching, teaching, preachers even; and of course here in our business and management worlds. One more thing there, when we as parents use the 'because I said so' reasoning, we are just the beginning stages of creating an adult down the road, who will resist change. Right? Of course, because for most of us, in all aspects of dealing with leaders our whole life, we were told, 'because I said so...trust me I know what's best ...do what I tell you,' and so forth.

Okay, so I am sure you are getting the message. You are not so resistant now because for two days you have had the opportunity to deal with reasoning, logic and to resolve the 'whys' in your mind?" Applause broke out and some verbal shouts of approval and understanding were heard.

We fully realize that we have not answered all of your questions, in fact, it's likely that none of your questions have been answered completely.

What we might have done is raised more questions in your mind, creating a thirst for more answers.

If that's the case, then we believe we have accomplished our goal. For, only by challenging our previous scope of reality and beliefs can we improve and change for the better.

On top of that, if we have learned, made some new relationships, stimulated our relationships, stimulated our thinking, and had some fun doing it, then we have achieved success.

It doesn't get any better than that!

As it all comes to an end, Booker shares some comments surrounding this last slide.

Judy Neu, who began the conference, quickly grabbed the attention of the crowd before Booker completely turned them loose, "One more time, please make sure you fill out your online critique and evaluation. We definitely want it. Just in case you have any troubles accessing, please just send me anything to the email address up there on the screen. You can always reach me here in Kansas City at that email; here if I can ever help your world. Look forward to your thoughts, and again thanks."

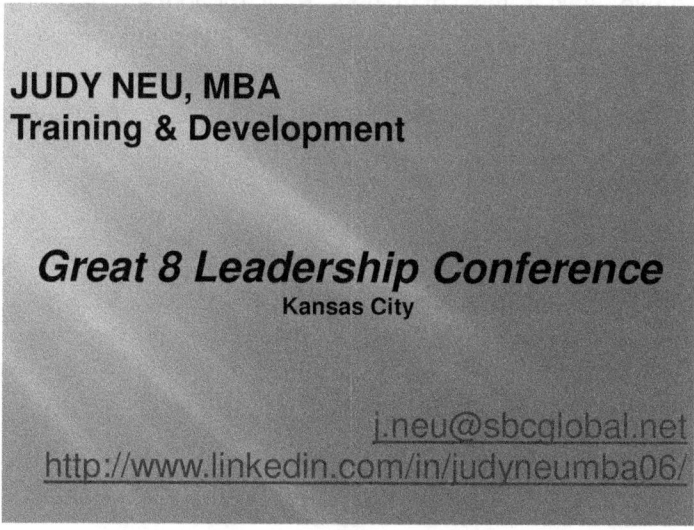

As people began to stand and mingle, both Debra and Les shook hands with some, exchanging some more business cards. They looked around for Mickey, who had left her seat; spotting her heading out the rear exterior doors. The two of them decided to sit right there and compare notes while they waited. As Debra scooted over a seat, set her purse and materials down, Les called Mickey on his cell. She was heading to the little girl's room having to go desperately; she was also going to talk to a couple of people, get some air and would meet them back in there. They sat and spoke about their learning for about 15 minutes before Mickey returned.

All facilitators were still up on stage, with several participants up there as well. Very few had actually left the auditorium at this point; lots of people actually spread out sitting and conversing about something or other.

Booker waves at everyone, "Hey, looks like I have lost control, so I will just say good bye again from all of us here. Feel free to hang out here as long as you wish. We have the place until 5:30pm. In case anyone's interested, most of us are going to meet over across the street at the Power & Light District for a cold one or whatever is your pleasure. Come join us; we'll be there until 7:30 and then we're going to scatter, head back homeward ourselves."

"God's very best to you and yours. Safe travels going home and if we don't connect again, please take care of those you lead and well....have a great life! And remember, we're always just a phone call away my friends."

After Action Report: Submitted to the CEO a Week Later

Debra took much time to think, bounce ideas off of others and reflect during that week upon return from the conference. Back into one routine, morning coffee times with Les took on some new dynamics and topics. She was taking some immediate and aggressive actions. With what she learned the past weekend she had to own up to her own shortcomings. She coordinated and did face to face talks with some peers; the HR Manager for sure and more than once gathered her own team to share and dialogue. Nearly always asking them for their thoughts first!

Before the conference, she would have never pictured herself doing any of that! Her insecurities would never have allowed her to open up as she was doing now. There were indeed some not helping immediately; but there were already positive signs. She had created this mess. Although some, subordinates and peers, were making this tough she was committed to becoming a real leader with solid relationships. People in her sphere had become a focus; they were now her 'job', she knew this now. They would become what would make her job a much better job...

As she had calculated throughout the conference, certain aspects of ROI were already coming to fruition. Over coming months, in quiet moments, she thought to herself, 'this stuff works'.

She smiled to herself as she sat down to start to type her trip report; Debra was actually eager to get this accomplished. Using notes she had taken there as well as over the last couple of days, she completed it over one day; it was emailed to the CEO, Les and a few others with whom she wanted to share.

At the end of the month, she emailed a personal note to Booker, as promised. Things were changing she assured him. His email response was nearly immediate, it simply read:

Debra,

Thanks for the note, very good to hear. As you know we are scheduled to visit/do some work with your company this fall. Appreciate the 'referral' and business for sure!

We Look forward to it and seeing you, Les and hopefully even Mickey again.

I am here if I can ever help. Absolutely enjoyed learning with you and all. Thanks for letting me abuse you up on the stage. Your words meant a lot to many sincerely; I have received many emails regarding your words (and tears) shared. Lastly, I want to share something that helped me at a tough time in life, and just thought you might appreciate, see attached.

God's best my friend,

**"People don't care how much you know
until they first know how much you care."**

Doug Booker
www.bookertraining.com
913.232.0244

Join me on **TWITTER**

Join me on **LINKED IN**

Join me on **FACEBOOK**

....blogging now at www.conferenceforleaders.com

Sometimes we come to life's crossroads and

we view what we think is the end,

But GOD has a much wider vision and he knows that it is

only a bend,

The road will go on and get smoother...and

after we have stopped for a rest,

The path that lies hidden beyond us,

is often the path that is best,

So rest and relax and get stronger,

let go and let GOD share your load,

And have faith in a brighter tomorrow,

You have just come to a bend in the road.

Helen Steiner Rice

Part of her report included some research. Debra had come across a concept called 'employee engagement' and its importance as well as symptoms of disengagement. One article she found stated "...Employee engagement is the cornerstone of achieving a sustainable competitive advantage." by Lee Colan, Ph.D. author of *Engaging the Hearts and Minds of all your Employees.*

She had found this within the McKinsey reports, as well. Dr. Colan identifies the symptoms and outcomes of this 'disengagement'. She decided to include the list as part of her trip report.

She knew she had disengagement with some of her people which was costing the company money; this she knew now for sure.

Debra had been a skeptic, and now she was a convert. She was determined to share her newfound belief in the ROI of developing leadership! She looked forward to growing and transforming herself as well. She was also a bit pumped to become a proponent for Women in Leadership, not just within her company, but externally as well, somehow.

She finished the report late after hours the Thursday upon return. As she was ready to hit the SEND button, one of her employees knocked and poked his head through the doorway, interrupting her thoughts. She thought momentarily how before today, she likely would have sent him away with some attitude possibly. Those days were done. She smiled, waving him to come in. She hit the SEND button, closed her laptop and walked around her desk to shake hands and focus on what would become a 'new & improved' relationship in her life! She had gotten the message it seemed.

Upon finally leaving, after helping him solve a little issue with some Fishing Teaching; a long day was done.

On her way out, she looked above the new meeting room she had transformed for her team. Above the doorway she had stenciled (using some of that new wall décor scripting). She was determined for this to become reality and not just be something on a wall!

Reminder to our Leaders & Team:

People don't care how much you know until, first, they know how much you care

Les opened his email the next morning, at the same time seeing the report which was lying there in hardcopy; placed in the center of his desk. This was also done for the CEO. Les's copy had not only Deb's signature scribbled at the bottom, but also a couple of words.

TO: CEO, Les & fellow LEADERS

    As many of you know, this past weekend I attended a management conference. To be completely candid I was not excited about going and considered any and all 'leadership training, conferences, retreats and all that' with disdain. Not only did I believe that I wouldn't learn anything, the thought of being away from work was causing me a lot of anxiety.
    Another thought was "why would we spend money on this type of training" as we all know how tight our budgets are?

    Let me tell you how wrong I was. Let me also assure you that this was not a 'management seminar,' but a Leadership Conference full of learning I intend to put to use for the company...and for ME!

    Those of you who know and have worked with me for awhile would probably describe me as pragmatic, driven and task oriented (not to mention a few other well-deserved names I am sure). While I cannot argue with those assessments I'd also add: 'value driven and fiscally conservative' into the conversation. The need to prove the value of any investment of time, energy or resources needs to be spelled out with a solid ROI before I would consider; that view and approach to things has not changed.

    However I do now view the investment in leadership development as having proven itself to have both a tangible ROI and significant intangible benefits as well. It has changed to the point I want every leader in the company to attend this training; or minimally to receive the content in productive and sustainable way! Leadership needs to become a priority throughout the organization.

You all are aware of the definition of business insanity: "Doing the same thing over and over again, and expecting different results".   I'll be the first to admit my guilt (you've never heard me say that before have you?) in some insane practices. With some modifications to our leadership approach we will reap the benefits of our measureable goals.

How you ask? The answers are: Trust, communication, feedback, coaching, and development, conflict resolution, relationship-building and much more. A structured, sustainable leadership process that allows us to remove barriers will have immediate results. Our key performance metrics of production, rework, missed delivery dates, absenteeism, and employee turnover will all be positively impacted.

Some of you likely don't buy into this right now. You will, trust me☺. There are some leadership points there, more on that later.

I have also realized we aren't alone - many organizations (maybe nearly all from my experiences) have these same types of issues. With real developmental training and focus on improved leaders, other companies have made improvements. There are industry reports from highly respected thought leaders such as McKinsey who support and document ROI for companies that invest in their employees. I am providing you a link here (https://www.mckinseyquarterly.com); for anyone interested in looking at all this further right now.

According to McKinsey, mentioned above, paraphrasing a bit, " To unlock a team's abilities, a manager at any level must spend a significant amount of time on two activities: helping the team understand the company's direction and its implications for team members and coaching for performance. Across industries, managers spend 30 to 60 percent of their time on administrative work and meetings, and 10 to 50 percent on non-managerial tasks (traveling, participating in training, taking breaks, conducting special projects, or undertaking direct customer service or sales themselves).

They spend only 10 to 40 percent actually managing (or leading) employees by; for example, coaching them directly. Yikes!!!!!!!!!!!!!!!!!!!! ...is what I say to that!

Remember when I said how wrong I was? I would not only have never said that before this past weekend, I would also never have admitted that I could be a better leader. Investing in sustained leadership development & training for the team, the entire chain of command is the most imperative strategic decision we *will* make this year.   I have much more research and ROI facts and information to share as we pursue all this soon. We must work to create a sustainable process that evolves from training to routine coaching by the leader's leader. This begins with tying leadership competencies and performance metrics to the development strategies and training curriculum. More on all this later...

I will leave you with a listing I found regarding the symptoms and outcomes of not having an engaged workforce (not involving those you and I lead):

"....Missed Deadlines, Low Morale, Increased Worker Comp claims, High Absenteeism, Call-in's, No-show's, Lack of Accountability,

Excuses, Lack of Responsibility, Apathy, Disregard of compliance and regulations, Gossip & Conflict, Low retention of high performers, High Turnover…"

Do the math, I have. This is a no-brainer; we must do this!

Respectfully, Debra

<u>Quote picked up at the Conference:</u>
"People don't care how much you know until first they know how much you care"

Les, this quote now says so much to me about leadership. You will find this in my signature block from now on; and I will ask you and others to hold me accountable to its intent in my own leadership behaviors!

THANX so much for making me go to that conference. ☺ You are a great boss and a great leader!

Deb

Some Questions to Ponder:

- What is it like to be managed by me?

- What am I expected to do and be as a manager?

- What do those I lead want and need from me?

- Do I like my people—each of them?

- Do my people like me and do I care if they do?

- What do I want in and from my own manager?

- What am I not getting that I would like?

- Do I seek out the wisdom of God in my daily walk as a leader?

- What am I getting that I don't want or like?

- What's my vision of and for the team I manage?

- What's my team's vision?

- What would it mean if that vision were achieved?

- Who holds me accountable for positive leadership (behavioral) change and improvement?

- Do you have someone(s) to whom you are accountable for your personal and professional life?

- Mentors are needed by everyone, do I have them and am I effectively mentoring others?

- What, if eliminated, would make productivity leap?

- What is working alright, but not making a positive difference?

- When was the last creativity initiative or idea that I led?

- How have the last significant changes gone on my team or in the organization?

- Are you normally 'telling' or 'teaching'....facilitating?

- What relationships, if improved, would make a positive impact on our team, the group I lead, or within/between departments?

- What is preventing effective communications among those I lead, and within the organization overall?

- Does our organization or department structure make sense to all (to you)?

Author and Coauthors

DOUG BOOKER

President and Founder of Booker Training Associates, Doug is a professional facilitator, change agent, coach, author/speaker and organizational developer. Booker Training Associates is a business that Doug began after a successful military career. In 1994 he retired from the Army (Infantry) at the rank of Major.

Booker is a strong believer in learning and preaches 'Never Stop Learning'. Following his own advice, he completed an Executive MBA, Lean Business certification and a Masters in Management; now in Ministry studies. He has worked with a variety of industries and teaches at four different graduate-level universities. Doug received the Army's Leadership (ROTC) Faculty of the Year award in 1989; receiving this recognition from the Secretary of Defense in Washington D.C.

The "associates" of Booker Training Associates are other experts he brings to the process, depending on the situation and assessed needs.

Doug has counterparts in all aspects of organizational dynamics: human resources, operations, quality, finance, marketing and more.

In his next book Doug is shifting gears by delving into his deep faith in God. He has already begun this endeavor by involving close family and friends in creating a 'dialogue' from many different perspectives about faith, Jesus, scriptures, our purpose, life, non-believers, the Word and other spiritual topics!

Doug regards his family - wife Sydney, his two children and parents - as the best parts of his life, along with being able to work in a field that he loves, helping people.

Doug's favorite quote, to which he asks people to hold him accountable, in life and work, is:

"People don't care how much you know until they first know how much you care"
(John Maxwell is whom he credits for this piece of wisdom)

****

I love people and I am passionate about helping leaders and organizations with their *people-systems*. I would love to hear from you about the book, the content here or *anything at anytime* my friend,

Doug Booker

www.bookertraining.com / www.theconferenceforleaders.com

913.232.0244 / doug@bookertraining.com

...on Facebook, Twitter, LinkedIn!

DEBRA HAYES, Lenexa, KS 66219
913.269.3634
dhayes66219@yahoo.com   www.linkedin.com/in/debrahayes

Getting people unstuck and helping them move their spot is what I do as a professional seminar leader, facilitator, trainer, motivational speaker, and life coach. The first step is having a clear understanding of where you are - or your business is - and what has been tried; then we get down to work. One of the biggest keys is looking at the habits, beliefs, attitudes, and expectations that are guiding your thoughts, feelings, and actions. Think of this as the "culture" of your life or company. Are they serving you or not serving you? How do you change them to serve you? If you knew how to move your spot, wouldn't you already be doing it?

The great news is, you CAN move your spot, change your life, be the person you REALLY are, do what REALLY makes you happy, and propel yourself and your business to success . . . and more.

Masters Degree from Rockhurst University (Executive Fellows Program); member of the following organizations: The Central Exchange / Society for Human Resource Management (SHRM) - national and local chapters (HRMAJC / HRMA of KC) / International Society for Performance Improvement (ISPI) / American Society for Training and Development (ASTD) - local chapter (KC ASTD) / Young Women on the Move (YWOM) / Life member - - Girl Scouts of the USA

TERRELL L. MCTYER, Kansas City, MO
Marketing@MIPromotions.com   http://www.MIPromotions.com
816.921.3633

Terrell L. McTyer (aka Terrell L) was born and raised in Kansas City, MO. He is the founder, CEO, and Lead Strategist of M/I Promotions and Marketing Excellence (www.MIPromotions.com). M/I is a full service marketing agency which also provides eblasts, promotions, social media marketing, branding, design, business development, product sales, event marketing and management, public relations, advertising, and booking for individuals, businesses, and ministries across the nation.

Terrell has a Business Management/Marketing degree from the University of Phoenix. His initial degree work was in Architectural Engineering/Construction Management at the University of Kansas. While in college he involved himself in many organizations including Alpha Phi Alpha Fraternity, Inc. and the National Society of Black Engineers. He also studied voice at the University of Missouri - Kansas City Conservatory of Music. Terrell has sang in many music groups, performed in operas and music theater, and written and recorded countless songs. He also founded the music ministry Called Out of Darkness (www.CalledOutOfDarkness.com)

Terrell is an ordained Elder of the Gospel, music recording artist, serial entrepreneur, counselor, and community leader. Above all, he is a loving husband and father to four beautiful children.

LES HYDE, Overland Park, Kansas
leshyde@gmail.com

Les Hyde has an extensive leadership background in customer service and IT operations. He has worked in diverse organizations including several private companies, two Fortune 500 companies, and the United States Air Force.

He holds a B.S. in Information Systems from Park University, an MBA from University of Phoenix, numerous technical certifications and is a Six Sigma Greenbelt. Les is passionate about the customer experience, and achieving sustainable and repeatable results through People, Process and Technology. He has served on several non-profit boards and volunteers his time to helping others.

Sponsors, Visitors, and Guests

(These are real people, real businesses, who would be happy for you to contact them!)

Warren Wandling

'We bring focus to your life...equipping leaders to multiply clients, revenue & productivity!'

913-406-9509

Awakeningsignificance.com

Booker & Golf Pro Darek Dubsky
www.bookertraining.com
816.522.1680

"We sell new & used books for your reading pleasure."

Tim Cash, Owner

tmcash@msn.com
816.659.4508

www.half.com, terylcosystems

Parker Business Change Solutions
PO Box 47403, Kansas City, MO 64188
(816) 582-4175

Web site: Parkerbcs.com
Email: David@Parkerbcs.com

"When leaders change, organizations change."

Financial Services!

- Life Insurance
- Investments
- Debt Solutions
- Identity Protection
- & More!

Tim Goodwin
508.499.9324
tgoodwin@primerica.com

Pastor Chauncey Dixon

Sr Pastor - Refiner's Fire World Outreach Center
Sr Pastor - First Baptist Church (Bonner Springs, KS)
227 Armour St,   Bonner Springs, KS 66012

913-244-9307 / cdixon@rfwoc.org

VIP TRAVELINKS

*Call us for all of your conference
or other business travel plans!
We can also plan your next vacation!*

Deb Stafford-Gray
913.334.5302
Viptravelinks@yahoo.com

Conference Evaluations, feedback or input to:

JUDY NEU, MBA
Training & Development

Great 8 Leadership Conference
Kansas City

j.neu@sbcglobal.net
http://www.linkedin.com/in/judyneumba06/

....or just contact the author of the book!   **Doug Booker**

www.bookertraining.com

913.232.0244 / doug@bookertraining.com

...also on: Facebook, Twitter, LinkedIn

"Thanks

for coming.

Please tell your

friends!"

www.ingramcontent.com/pod-product-compliance
Lightning Source LLC
Chambersburg PA
CBHW071406170526
45165CB00001B/197